Broken
SPIRIT

*He healeth the broken in heart,
and bindeth up their wounds.*

PSALMS 147:3

Rose Jackson-Beavers

Published by Prioritybooks Publications
Florissant, Missouri

P. O. Box 2535
Florissant, Mo 63033
Copyright ©2018 by Rose Jackson-Beavers

All scriptures are taken from the King James Version of the Holy Bible.

This book is a work of fiction. The incidents, characters, and dialogue are products of the author's imagination and are not to be interpreted as real. Any resemblance to actual people, living or dead, is entirely coincidental.

Edited by: Kendra Koger, LaMia L. Ashley and Sheliawritesbooks

Cover Designed by Brittani Williams
Manufactured in the United States of America
Library of Congress Control Number: 2017944190
ISBN: 9780989650298

For information regarding discounts for bulk purchases, please contact Prioritybooks Publications at 1-314-306-2972 or rosbeav03@yahoo.com.

Dedication

To my mom, Connie Mae Booker, you are my world, and I appreciate your tender loving care. I will always love you. May God bless you always!

Chapter One

*B*ouncing and singing to the melodic grooves of Al Green, Stephanie was cheerful and in love. She knew every word to the song Al sang with perfection and confidence. She enjoyed singing the lyrics to "I'm Still in Love with You," her jam. Stephanie loved Al Green and listened to 100.3 The Beat, while singing her heart out. She popped her fingers and sang with her loud, alto voice vibrating throughout the car, putting her all into the song.

Excited about the prospect of seeing her man, Stephanie shimmied and danced to the song's beat. She missed Donnie and couldn't wait to see him.

Everyone considered Donnie Johnson a charmer. Stephanie met him two years ago at a charity affair for a mentoring program. He was a new manager, recently hired, at a local computer firm that had sent several of their managers to donate time and money to help the cause of keeping troubled teens out of jail by providing them with opportunities to work with professionals.

Donnie was a 32-year-old, six foot, bald-headed, caramel-colored brother who favored tailored suits and pressed, crisp, white shirts with neckties that blended well with his colors. He looked exquisite and reeked of money and good fortune. Plus, he had a mellow voice that transported unsuspecting females out of their underwear and into his bed without them realizing what happened.

After dating Stephanie for over a year, exclusively, he presented her with a flawless, white, four karats, square-cut diamond and asked her to marry him. She agreed. Now, their scheduled day to tie the knot was two weeks away.

As Stephanie turned into the Ridge Park subdivision, with its newly-built, two story, ranch-style, brick homes, the sound of her ringing phone interrupted her thoughts. She turned the music down and grabbed her cell off the passenger seat. She recognized the picture of her best friend's smiling face, as the name Regina and her number flashed on the screen. Stephanie smiled and pressed the answer button.

"Hey, girl." Regina's unmistakable voice filled her car. "What's up?"

The two friends met 20 years ago, at a Christian function. Regina Wilcox visited her church and they happened to sit together. They ended up chatting and exchanging phone numbers. The two girls were totally opposite of each other. While Stephanie flaunted a huge smile with perfect, white teeth and was considered by many as a beautiful, mocha-colored, brown-eyed girl with extremely long hair, who barely stood 5'4 in her clunky pumps, Regina was a gorgeous Caucasian, standing 5'6 and skinny with giraffe-like long legs that seemed to go on for miles.

The color of her hair served up a dark blond color, and her crystal blue eyes sparkled reminiscent of the sky. They reminded you of the clear, blue waters rolling up on the beach and cascading back into the ocean.

Both girls were beautiful. Stephanie's big ol' trusting heart seemingly got her in trouble. Always a friend to everyone, and even when someone hurt her, she would accept apologies and move on. Regina, on the other hand, was honest, critical of others, and held grudges. When they met, they were 11-years-old and just starting to wear clunky heels and the wrong color makeup and lipstick. But once they exchanged phone numbers, they became inseparable, even attending the same college and sharing rooms. These two ladies were thick as 20-year-old tree barks and stood together on issues even if the other wasn't too keen on the situation. They both came from upper middle class, educated parents and lived about 15 minut/ other.

The day they met, Regina's church visited Steph. gation to participate in a concert as special guests. Tha beginning of an honest and beautiful relationship. Both girls with their share of problems, bad boyfriends, and teary nights on the phone; but when things boiled down, they always counted on each other. While in college, Regina's family packed up and moved to Fort Meyers, Florida. But Regina accepted a job with a large, St. Louis firm as an attorney, which made Stephanie happy because she started her nonprofit company in the same area.

"Hey, Regina, girl, are you back in town?"

"Not yet. I'm still in Florida. I changed my plan due to a delay and won't return until next week sometime. My siblings want me to stay a little longer, since we haven't seen each other in a while." Regina pulled down her rearview mirror and wiped the excess lipstick from the corners of her mouth.

Turning her head to check out the homes in their new subdivision, Stephanie asked, "Well, how's your mom?"

"She's good, and she told me to tell you hi, and she'll contact you in two weeks." Smiling at her reflection in the mirror, Regina tilted the mirror up and focused on the road ahead of her.

"That's good. I cannot wait to see Mrs. Wilcox again. How many years has it been since I've seen her? Too many. I love your mom."

Frowning before responding, Regina stated, "Too bad Momma has to come to this wedding of yours to witness this travesty. I wish you would take my advice and not marry that fool."

"I still don't understand why you don't like him. He does so much good for the children and young men at the boys' club. He spends hours helping them with their homework and teaching them how to be good, young men."

"But, Stephanie, your problem is being blind. I'm concerned by what you're not recognizing, and that bothers me. Remember that time you brought him to your company's party and he tried to talk *ne* of your friends?"

"He said he was playing." Stephanie rubbed the side of her face. The conversation was bothering her. She didn't want to remember the negative stuff.

Slapping her steering wheel in frustration, Regina asked, "What would you say if you were caught, red-handed, trying to talk to another woman?"

"Well, that happened then, and this is now. Donnie asked me to marry him and not anyone else. So, my dear best friend, although I love you dearly, please understand this is my decision and accept the situation."

"I am your best friend, which is why I have tried my darnedest to stop this. But, I'll leave your wedding alone. You, and only you, will have to live with your decision. I'll be here when you need me."

"That's all I ask, Regina. I just want you to support me. I'm happy, and that's all that should matter."

"I'll let you have this one, but the next time-"

"It won't be one, Regina, so let this go, please."

"I gotta go, girl, but I'll call you when I come to town next week. Be good; I love you."

"Love you too, girl. Smooches."

Stephanie pressed end call on her phone and sat the phone back into the cradle on her car's dashboard. She smiled, thinking about the conversation. One thing she liked about Regina was her honesty.

Stephanie laughed as she drove through the subdivision. She lived in a beautiful area, but she and Donnie decided to sell their homes and purchase one together. They put their homes on the market and they would be on display throughout the month. They hoped someone would buy them quickly. Stephanie was ecstatic about a house she'd found and couldn't wait for her fiancé to view the structure.

She remembered the day clearly. *"Donnie, let's check out this house in that new subdivision we passed the other day."*

He reached over as he drove and squeezed her thigh. "If you let me bless you with some good loving when we arrive, I'll be happy to take a look."

"Boy, you silly if you think I'm going to lay on some filthy floor folks been walking over."

"You want me like I do you, right? I love you." He turned his head slightly to glance into her eyes.

"Boy, you better put your eyes back on the road." Stephanie took her two forefingers and pointed from her eyes to the street. "You better listen to me. Ain't nobody got time for car accidents."

"Girl, you feening for what I'm going to do to you?"

"I can't wait." Stephanie squeezed Donnie's right hand and smiled. Happy and satisfied, things in her life were materializing the way she always dreamed they would.

Stephanie couldn't wait to sign the papers for the house they were going to buy together. About to visit Donnie's home, Stephanie drove up to the white, chain link fence with the multi-colored daisies peeking throughout multiple links. As she stepped out of her white BMW, she passed by the red, yellow, and pink flowers and leaned over to sniff the sweet fragrance lingering in the air. Stephanie stood up straight, tossed her thick, shoulder-length, auburn-colored hair back into the wind and strutted to the front door of the house to locate the man she would marry in two weeks. She used her key to open the front door. Stephanie was going to surprise her fiancé, who had no idea his lady had arrived home early from a business meeting in Los Angeles.

Stephanie was a day early, and she had missed him so much that she traded her seat for one on standby, just to arrive early enough to rush to the man who would soon become her life partner. She was excited because she had not seen him in five days. That's how long she counted since they had kissed or touched each other; she was excited to feel his loving arms wrapped around her waist as they became one.

Stephanie walked through the house with her white, 4-inch, crystal-covered sandals silently clicking on the beige carpet. She stopped and stood in the foyer, looking in the mirror to give herself a once-over before seeing him. Placing her Fendi, calfskin bag and car keys on the Balbo console table, she primped and turned to check out her appearance in the circular mirror. Her white, sheath dress that hugged her body emphasized her small waist and her sexy breasts that were deemed 'just right' by Donnie. Stephanie was gorgeous, but not conceited, and understood how to handle her looks. Although a sharp dresser, she focused more on her education and her work. Stephanie was grateful she didn't have a weight problem, but she was careful to present the right attitude of someone who was appreciative of life and charitable to others. Her parents had always taught her, in life, you attract more with sugar than salt. Her efforts to focus on her heart had always made her stand taller amongst her colleagues and others. She inspected herself in the mirror to ensure her appearance would be appreciated by her man who loved to flaunt beautiful women on his arm.

Pivoting, she walked toward the en-suite. She noted Donnie's Land Rover parked in the driveway when she pulled up to the fence. He was home. Since she had not bumped into him or detected any movement, she assumed he was in the bedroom. As she moved closer to their special spot, she heard their song blaring, which made her feel all joyful and unique inside.

It was their signature song, "The Point of it All," by singer, Anthony Hamilton. She practically jogged to the bedroom, thinking about what would be happening in 2.5 seconds. As she touched the doorknob, she heard something knocking up against the wall. Twisting the doorknob, Stephanie nearly choked on the gum she was chewing.

"Oh, baby, your stuff is so good to me. Do your thing, girl." Donnie huffed and grunted out of breath.

"I love you." A woman, with her long legs wrapped around Donnie's back, screamed out as he pounded into her.

"Aww, baby. Don't stop." Donnie was thrusting himself into the woman, as if he had never experienced anything so good in his life. If Stephanie didn't know any better, she would think the man was crying.

The two, whipped fools sweet-talked and moaned so loudly over the music, they never even spotted her standing directly over their heads. Stephanie allowed the tears to pour from her eyes, as she searched the room for something to grab. The sting of betrayal begged her to kill Donnie. Not only that, he had mocked her by having sex with another woman while their song played in the background. Her heart pained with hurt and the feeling of rejection. She wanted to hurt him and make him experience the pangs of a broken heart like she was experiencing. Noticing the fireplace, she reached for the fireplace poker and walked in slow motion toward the man who had just crushed her heart. Lifting the poker up into the air, she slammed the deadly weapon across his head. Blood spurted out and spread quickly onto the screaming woman, who jumped out of bed and tried to run, but Stephanie was right behind her.

"Please don't hurt me. Please." The young lady looked no more than 20 years old. Her eyes bucked, and she looked like a deer blinded by headlights that was about to get hit by a speeding car. She looked terrified. Her straight, blond hair stood straight up on her head. Fear had caused her muscles to throb under her skin. Her pores began to exude sweat, and the hair on her arms, back, and neck started to stand up after seeing Stephanie swing the poker and strike Donnie with a violent blow to his head. The woman's entire body and brain were stimulated by fear. The young lady used her hands to hide her pale, white breasts, full, pink nipples and her private area, but her actions failed to cover her up. "I don't understand what's going on." She was inching toward the wall and reaching for her clothing. "Please, for God's sake, don't kill me. Who are you?" She cried. "Why are you doing this to us?"

"The question is, why are you in my fiancé's bed having sex with the man I am scheduled to marry in two weeks?"

Searching for her clothes, she stayed as far away from the crazed woman who was wielding a poker with a desperate look of anger and hate etched across her face. "This is my boyfriend." The lady screamed, as if she had been hit by a car. She slid her long, skinny, white body down the cream-painted wall; once on the floor, she scooted across the hickory hardwood to secure her dress that was bunched up in the corner. "Please don't beat me," she sobbed.

"You mean like you're doing me, slut?" Stephanie gripped the long, black, body of the poker and swung at the lamp on the table, which broke into tiny pieces while crashing to the ground.

The sound of the table lamp hitting the floor terrified the girl, and she pled for the stranger to let her go. "Please, lady, let me go. I don't know you, and I don't want to die."

"I'm not going to hurt you. But this two-timing fool over there, I am going to beat the mess out of him."

Pivoting around to focus on the one person she trusted, she tried to hold back her anger. A surge of hate and disgust so powerful consumed her body and thoughts that she believed she would die from the energy in the room. She rushed to the bed where Donnie lay bleeding to finish him off. Stephanie raised the poker and Donnie's eyes fluttered open. He jerked to full attention and rolled off the bed. As he tried to stand up, he staggered like a drunkard leaving a bar.

"Are you crazy, Steph?" He shook his head to gather his senses. Donnie asked and grabbed a towel off the chair next to the bed, pressing down on his head to halt the bleeding. He walked toward Stephanie with his other hand raised. "Please, baby, this means nothing."

Seeing his private member dangling made her madder. With her left hand, she covered her left ear, as if she was trying to block out the noise. She was about to hit him again when she caught a voice saying: *Don't do this;* it's not worth jail. Stephanie. Put the poker down and flee.

"No." She screamed, as she swung the poker up into the air, missing Donnie. But before she brought the poker down again, the voice interrupted, *Flee, Stephanie; now.*

Dropping the poker, she turned and sprinted to the front of the house, grabbed her purse and keys off the table, opened the door, ran to the car, and jumped inside. She made it safely and locked the door as Donnie, who was running behind her, almost on her heels, took a brick and tried to break her window. He was screaming like a person suffering from behavioral issues, as he chased the car, naked, with the towel still pressed against his head.

The car was speeding out of control as Stephanie pressed the accelerator as hard as she could. She looked out of her rearview mirror and realized Donnie had stopped and wrapped the towel he used to wipe the blood from his head wound around his waist as a small crowd started to gather.

Stephanie was despondent. All she could think about was killing herself. She could not believe this was happening to her. She thought she had found the one - the man of her dreams. She thought she could trust him, but like all the rest, he was a liar and a lust-filled idiot. He didn't wear a condom. How many times had he exposed her to diseases?

Kill yourself, an obnoxious-sounding voice barked. *Don't nobody want you. You keep getting hurt. Life isn't worth it.*

She hit the steering wheel so hard she injured her hand, which only made her cry harder as she tried to shake away the pain. "Please, God, please help me."

Chapter Two

"Get off at the next highway exit and go to the church at the end of the block." The voice was so smooth, if she hadn't been so hurt and out of control, she'd have slipped into a deep sleep from the soothing sound. "Ask for the pastor."

"What?" Did she hear that right?

"Exit now." The soothing voice commanded.

Stephanie almost passed the exit and quickly jerked to the right, turning off the highway. "What do I do, what do I do?" Her voice was husky and shaken. She was in shock. Scared. Confused.

"Go to the church and ask for the pastor. He will understand what to do," the calm voice said. It settled her spirit.

Stephanie drove onto the lawn of the church. With no available parking spaces in sight, she decided to park wherever she found an empty space. She wondered what was going on; maybe a funeral or wedding, but she pulled up and came to an abrupt stop.

"Why are so many cars at this place on a Saturday?" she said out loud. The sun beamed down on her tear-stained face. Not yet 2:00, it was already hot and sticky. At almost 95 degrees, her dress stuck to the back of her thighs, as she jumped out of her car and dashed into the church, passing people mulling through the vestibule. Stephanie didn't care that she'd left her car running with the door open.

Storming inside, she shouted, "I'm looking for the pastor. Somebody, please help me. Where is the pastor?"

People turned to stare at her. Two tall men in black suits rushed to her side. "Young lady, may we help you?"

"I need to see your pastor. Please. I need help." Tears streamed down her face as her hair stood all over her head due to the wind from the highway tossing her strands everywhere. She looked like a beautiful woman in distress, as she rushed through another set of doors in the church. "Please, find me the pastor."

"Who are you and why do you want the pastor?" The pecan-colored man asked. "We can help you. What's the problem?" he asked as other people began to gather around them and Stephanie.

Starting to hyperventilate, she responded, "I can't breathe."

Just then, a medium height man, who was better looking than Lance Gross, the actor, pushed through the crowd of people and grabbed her hand. "Come with me."

Elder Brown said, "Pastor, one of the church members said she left her car running with her purse inside."

"Please, take care of that for me." The handsome pastor directed then turned to focus his attention on the distraught young woman. He and the second elder walked with her between them to the pastor's study. The pastor closed the door and turned to look at her. "Young lady, we are here to help. Tell me, what is the problem?"

"I want to kill myself. My heart hurts. He broke my heart. Help me, so I won't do anything stupid. I don't want to die. I think the devil is trying to make me harm myself."

"What is your name?"

"Stephanie Whitmore."

"Ms. Whitmore, let's pray." The pastor gently pulled Stephanie to her knees with him. Elder Jim Duncan joined them. He took her hands into his and bowed his head. Elder Duncan placed his hands on Stephanie's shoulder and the back of the pastor. "Lord, you have brought your wounded child to our doors. We ask You, Lord, to help us guide her and show her that today she did the best thing possible to provide her with life. She came to Your house. In Your house, there is peace, love, and understanding. Lord, we ask You to take care of this young woman who is seeking solace and help to prevent her from hurting herself. She has come to You through us, but we have faith, Lord, only You will show her the way. You brought her here for a purpose. Let us help her the way You want us to. Let whatever problems that are affecting her be lifted. Lord, we experienced your miracles. Save her from herself and her pain. Allow her to call on You to save her. She took an important step. Keep her mind open so we can continue to provide her with the help she is seeking through Your name. Lord, we ask You to guide all of us appropriately to give Stephanie Whitmore what she needs. Let her be wise enough that we will be able to help her. Bless her, help us, and feed her with the Holy Spirit. I pray that You will strengthen me to help. In Jesus' name we pray. Amen."

Pastor Daniel Winston helped Stephanie up and led her to the couch. "Please, tell me what is hurting you." The elder sat in the chair opposite the sofa.

She took a deep breath and bent her head down into her open hand. As she sat there, the pastor observed the small flecks of red on her white dress, which looked like blood.

"Take your time."

"I've been waiting all my life to find the man of my dreams and I thought I found him. In two weeks, I was getting married. Today, I arrived at my fiancé's house from a business trip in Los Angeles. I planned to surprise him. But lo and behold, the surprise was on me. I walked into his bedroom to find him in bed with a woman."

Hoping she didn't kill the couple, he asked, "What happened next?"

"I took the fireplace poker and hit him in the head as hard as my strength would permit."

"Is he alive?"

"Yes, he is. I mean, he chased me, naked and bleeding, to my car." She laughed. "Pastor, can you imagine seeing a grown, naked man chasing a woman because she caught him in the wrong?"

The pastor smiled, but he didn't say anything.

"I wanted to kill him but the voice wouldn't let me."

"What voice?"

"The one that told me not to kill him because jail and murder weren't worth it, and to flee to this church. It told me to ask for you, the pastor."

"The voice of God."

"I think." She, again, laid her head into her hands and cried. The pastor rubbed her back until she composed herself enough to speak.

"I spent nearly 30 thousand dollars on this wedding. It's a mess. I don't even know where to start. I must contact people and cancel products. All my money... wasted."

"Some of the vendors will give you some of the money back, minus the deposits. I realize the money is significant, but at least you won't be stuck in a marriage that is not sanctioned by God."

"What makes you think it's not sanctioned by God?"

Before the pastor could respond, Stephanie spoke. "Well, you're right. A relationship sanctioned by God wouldn't have me sitting here crying like this, and we aren't even married yet."

She stood up and paced back and forth on the royal blue carpet. "What am I going to do, Pastor? I'm sorry. What is your name?"

"Pastor Daniel Winston."

She sat back down on the couch next to him. "Thank you for listening to me. I just... I have never experienced this kind of hurt in my life. Why, Pastor? Why do men cheat on people they profess to love?"

"I cannot answer that for you. What I can say is that many men don't cheat. I also believe that when people live by the Bible and believe in God, they work hard to obey His commandments. When people don't have a strong relationship with God, yes, they may indeed cheat."

"I don't get it. I didn't ask him to marry me. He asked. I will never forgive him."

"I understand your pain. At this time, it might not be easy to see yourself forgiving someone who's hurt you. But the Bible says in Ephesians 4:32: 'And be ye kind one to another, tenderhearted, forgiving one another, even as God for Christ's sake hath forgiven you.' God forgives us, and he wants us to do the same for others."

"I cannot see that happening. This man put my life in danger with his philandering ways. There are all kinds of diseases and crazy folks out here. Still, he let his desires think for him. But maybe it isn't lust. Maybe he's in love with her." Stephanie started to cry again. "I'm so sorry, Pastor, to bring this mess to you and your church. My heart hurts. I can't handle much more."

"Give it to God. Cast your burdens on Him. In Psalm 55:22, God says, 'cast thy burden upon the Lord, and He shall sustain thee: He shall never suffer the righteous to be moved.' What this means, Stephanie, is that God will support you, and He will never allow the righteous to be shaken. Do you believe that God will take care of you, Stephanie?"

"Yes, Pastor. I believe."

"Do you feel better? I mean, do you think you still want to die?"

Stephanie looked into the pastor's eyes and she saw so much compassion. There was a calmness that gave her comfort.

"No, I want to live. I won't let something like this kill me."

There was a knock at the door, and Elder Duncan answered it. Elder Brown walked in with Stephanie's purse and keys.

"I parked the car and here are your things."

"Thank you." Stephanie stood to leave. "Thank you so much, Pastor Winston. Thank you for listening to me."

"Please, I would like your phone number so that I can check on you from time to time. Is that okay with you?" The pastor asked, as he stared into her pretty eyes and almost lost his train of thought.

"Yes. Is your cellphone with you? I can put my number in." She waited.

The pastor reached into his pocket and took his phone out. He entered a password and handed it to Stephanie. They both jumped when their hands connected. "You shocked me." They both said it in unison.

"Are you okay?" The pastor asked her, as he reached over and touched her shoulder.

"Yes."

As Stephanie Whitmore typed her phone number into the pastor's phone, she also called out the digits. Elder Duncan wrote them down. She handed the pastor his phone back.

Pastor Winston reached for the phone and said, "May I make a suggestion?"

She looked at him with weary eyes. "What is it?"

"I think you should put in a request for an order of protection. Especially, since you injured your fiancé. It is likely he is going to reach out to you in some way."

"Yes, Pastor. I will go to the police department now and complete a report."

"I pray we have been helpful to you."

"Thank you, Pastor. Your help is appreciated."

"Are there any friends or family members available who you can go to for help when you leave here?"

"No. My parents are out of the country and my best friend is out-of-town. But I'll be fine. Thank you, again."

"May we say a final word of prayer?"

The pastor and the two elders circled Stephanie and prayed for her protection and asked God to watch over her. They asked God to touch her and bring her closer to Him. After the prayer, they invited her to visit the church and promised to stay in touch.

Stephanie walked out the door with Elder Brown, who agreed to show her where he'd parked her car. She twirled her body around to glance at the pastor again. He was handsome. She noticed his eyes, which never disconnected from hers, sparkle. She smiled and he returned the most heartfelt smile back. She felt his smile reach her heart. Suddenly, her burden seemed lifted.

When Stephanie pulled off the parking lot, she felt light. If she didn't know any better, she would have thought she lost 100 pounds. Maybe she did. Her wedding would never take place, and nothing would change that. Her life changed in less than two hours. What floated through her mind was if it would be for better or worse.

Chapter Three

"Elders, can you imagine what just happened here? God is amazing. He sent a young lady in despair off the highway to receive a message of hope and love from us. God works in mysterious ways."

"That's right, Pastor," Elder Brown said, taking a seat in the leather chair next to the pastor's massive, burgundy desk.

"Imagine how devastating that is to walk in on your soon-to-be husband."

Elder Duncan laughed heartily. "That brother is blessed. She hit him in the head with an iron poker stick. He is blessed to still be among the living."

"I'm happy nothing worse happened to him. Her life could've been ruined if he had died. She doesn't strike me as a person who means harm. Very classy lady... I got the impression she's been in church most of her life. She had that presence about her."

"You're right, Pastor. I got that feeling too. She's young, and she appears to be well-off. That car was a BMW 750Li Sedan. She pulled that car up on the grass like someone was chasing her, and left the keys and her purse in it. God was blessing her today. In this neighborhood, somebody would have had the car in no time and would've been gone. God is good." Elder Brown slapped his leg.

"My heart aches for her. To witness your life change like that in a few minutes. One minute, the world is in your hand, and the next, you're devastated. I'm sure she would give that car up for peace, love, and happiness." The pastor picked up his phone to check whether her phone number saved in his phone. Seeing her name and the number, he smiled.

"I wonder why men have affairs on such beautiful women, myself." Elder Duncan stood up to leave.

Elder Brown thought about a time in his life when he did the same thing.

"They do it because they can. Most of the time, they walk back in freely with the woman. But I can tell you this, when she slung that poker upside his head, he knew it was over with her. He played on the wrong one. Trust and believe though, he is going to try his darnedest to woo that one back. He's a fool, if he doesn't."

As the three men walked out the pastoral office, the pastor said, "I pray that it's over. As a matter-of-fact, Elder Duncan, I think we should visit her when the Sabbath is over. Is that okay with you?"

"Be careful, Pastor. She is getting out of a relationship, and I don't want your feelings hurt."

"What would make you think that I'm interested in a relationship with a person whose spirit is so broken? Plus, Elder, when God sends me a woman to be my wife, I'll discern it. In the meantime, this broken spirit needs all the spiritual help and encouragement we can give her."

"I'm just saying, Pastor, she is beautiful, and I sense something there."

"Something like what? She came to us for help and God led her here, and that's what we are going to give her. Understand?"

"Yes, and so it will be."

****

"Hi, Pastor."

"Hello, Sister Green. How are you on this beautiful Sabbath?"

"I'm doing great. I wanted you to meet a visitor who worshiped with us today. Sister Clay, this is our wonderful pastor, Daniel Winston."

"Hi, Pastor Winston. I enjoyed your sermon."

"Thank you for visiting with us today. We pray you will return."

"I will."

"Where is your church home?"

"I'm a member of The True Church with Pastor James Davis. However, I'm searching for a new church home."

"Pastor Davis is a friend of mine. He's a good man."

"Whatever you say, Pastor. Whatever you say." Sister Clay twisted her head around and rolled her eyes to the top of her head, making all kinds of faces. She was huffing and puffing like a five-year-old.

"Well, it was nice meeting you. Please, come again."

The pastor walked away, then looked back once more at Sister Clay and turned to Elder Brown. "Oh, Lord, have mercy on us."

"Wow, Pastor, I pray the devil don't find a way to prey on our church."

"Well, Elder Brown, you know the devil is busy. We'll need to stay in prayer," Pastor stated as the two men began to walk toward Pastor Winston's office.

"By the way, Elder Brown, after the Sabbath, I would like to check on Sister Stephanie Whitmore to make sure all is well with her. We need to encourage her to reach out to a family member. She was too distraught to handle her burdens without a family member to help her."

"After Sabbath, we can ride over together. I'll call for her address."

"Thanks, Elder. I'm going to stay and eat dinner in the fellowship hall. Come join me."

"I was on my way there."

****

"Sister Green, that church I came from ain't nothing but the devil. That pastor was over there sleeping with his members. I had to get out of there," Sister Clay said while shaking her head.

"Sister Clay, if that is true, you did the right thing by looking for a new church home. Ain't nobody got time to be worshipping under an unsaved pastor. Our salvation is too important. You will find that Pastor Winston is the real deal. He's a holy man who is serious about his salvation."

"Well, Sister, I shole hope so. But after seeing that damsel in despair running up in here with her hair blowing all over her head and with speckles of blood on that tight white dress, I'm gon' wait before I make my assessment."

"Lord, have mercy. Hush, Sister." Sister Green lifted her finger to her mouth to indicate to be quiet and speak carefully. "We don't play that at this church. We love our neighbors and friends, but if they come to do us harm, we will send them packing with a prayer."

"Well, I'm going to go and eat dinner and fellowship with your members. Come on, girl. Let's eat."

Grabbing Sister Clay's hand, Sister Green asked, "May I pray with you right now?"

Sister Clay pulled her hand out of Sister Green's and shook it like she was shaking the dirt off her.

"Girl, we can pray over dinner. Let's go."

"Lord Jesus, another test is coming. Prepare us, O' Lord, for the storm ahead." Sister Green quickly bowed her head and whispered to God, then she walked behind Sister Clay and followed her to the fellowship hall.

"Help us, Lord. Help us now."

****

Later that evening, after church service Elder Brown approached the pastor. "Pastor, I called Sister Whitmore and informed her we're coming over. I asked if she had eaten and she said no. We discussed her favorite foods, and she said she would love pasta and broccoli, so

I ordered her dinner, to go, from Applebee's. The restaurant is not too far from her home."

"That's very kind of you, Elder Brown. Thank you for being so considerate."

Elder Brown and Pastor Winston strutted to the car, amid stares and women stopping to ask questions. Eventually, they succeeded in getting to the car and left. Elder Brown maneuvered his new Buick LaCrosse like a champion chess player who avoided showing his next move. Women stood in the parking lot, admiring the handsome, single men and weren't too eager to move out of their view.

"How do you avoid all these beautiful women trying to acquire your attention?" Elder Brown turned slightly toward the pastor but he never took his eyes off the road. He wanted to understand because of his status of being single and dating. He often found himself in trouble with the women he dated. Now committed to just one woman, women often pursued him.

"Prayer. God called me to teach and preach. God called me to spread the message of salvation, and the day I can no longer do that, I will leave the pulpit."

"But, Pastor, these women call you throughout the night, showing up at your home unannounced, bringing you all kinds of desserts and gifts, willing to do anything for you. Yet, you smile and tell them you cannot accept their gifts and move forward. Honestly, some of these women are gorgeous."

"Think about how you stay clean. What do you do?" Pastor Winton smiled, showing pearly white, polished teeth.

"I pray and lean on my girlfriend. She understands. But I'm not going to lie, I still find it quite difficult to fight the temptation."

"I'm sure most men suffer the same problems. But when you think about all the problems and trouble it would cause to step out, it's a little easier to be careful."

"Check this out, Pastor. A young woman asked me to give you this letter."

Pastor Winston reached over and took the letter. He opened the envelope at the corner. He pulled the paper all the way down the side, making the envelope look unopened. Pastor Winston removed the letter and unfolded the paper. He chuckled after he read the content. Then he read it out loud.

"Pastor, I wanted to ask if you would be interested in accompanying me to the theater to watch The Wiz. I would love for you to be my guest. Afterward, you can sample the dessert I made for you. Please contact me as soon as possible so I can pick up the tickets. Sister K. Johnson."

"Oh, so she's going to allow you to sample her dessert. How can you turn her down?" Elder Brown laughed.

"This is what I tried to tell you. If I sampled all the desserts I'm offered, I would be fat, tired, and bothered with a lot of little children running around the church calling me Daddy. Now, tell me who would respect me then? Who would want a leader of a church who cannot resist temptation? I wouldn't. I would be embarrassed to say that's my pastor."

"That's what I mean… the stress of avoiding problems." Elder Brown shook his head, as he steered the car into a parking space at Applebee's.

"Lord, I'm so glad to be saved. I couldn't handle all those invitations. I love God too much to allow the earthly flesh to entice me. Sending invitations and personal invites are the last things to cause me to sin. Now, I'm not perfect, because none of us are, but I stay on my knees asking God to help me."

"Well, God called the right man for the right job. Pastor, I've never seen anything like what you experience." He pulled into a parking space and said, "I'll leave the air on while I run in to obtain Sister Whitmore's order."

"Hold on a second and stay here while I call and decline the date." The pastor called Sister Johnson and declined the date.

"I overheard her say you hurt her feelings, but maybe next time. You indicated to her that you didn't have any available time in the future, yet she invited you to something else, and she kept trying to force you to accept something. You would think she would grasp the message. These ladies are something else."

"But my God is smarter and so much wiser."

"Yes, indeed." Elder Brown said, as he got out the car and entered the restaurant.

Chapter Four

*T*hey arrived at Stephanie Whitmore's ranch-style home in Florissant, Missouri. She stayed in a community with newer-styled ranch and two-story homes. Her BMW was parked in her circular driveway. They parked behind her car, got out, and strolled to the door. Elder knocked with his right fist, as he held the bag of food in his left hand.

"Why don't you ring the doorbell?" The pastor asked.

"Didn't see it." He pushed the bell this time and the door swung open. Stephanie looked distraught; her long hair stuck up like she'd been lying down on her head. The red dress highlighted her mocha-colored skin, which reminded the Pastor of a creamy, brown, chocolate color. She stepped back. "Please, come in."

The pastor needed to hug her. He walked over. "How are you today?"

"I'm much better."

He embraced her, as did Elder Brown.

"We brought you something to eat." The Elder said.

She took the bag and said, "Thank you so much. Please, take a seat in the living room."

Stephanie turned and took the bag to the kitchen. When she returned, she sat on the loveseat across from the two handsome brothers.

"I want to thank you both for your help today. I arrived at the church in a mess. Honestly, I still am, but with God's help, I will survive this. So, I'm better than before, but I hurt like I never have."

The pastor leaned forward. "You're going through a season, and in time, this will pass. We came by to pray for you and to check on you. Have you contacted any family members who can be here for you?"

"No. My parents are still out of the country and my best friend is in Florida. I can handle this."

"Did you speak to the young man?"

"No. He's been calling, but that's over."

Pastor Winston couldn't find the words to help her. He appeared star struck or something. He just sat staring at Stephanie. Elder Brown observed the always talkative pastor looking out of sorts and decided to spearhead the meeting.

"We are not going to stay long. We just wanted to bring you something to eat and pray for you. Do you mind?"

"Of course not. Please pray for me."

Elder Brown led the prayer and filled the room with peace and calmness. The atmosphere gave off an aroma like the Holy Ghost snuck in the room. Stephanie started crying and whispering, 'Thank you, Jesus.' Elder Brown embraced her after the prayer and asked her to call if she needed anything. He reminded her that he and the Bible workers would be visiting her again.

Before leaving, Pastor Winston finally found his voice. He reminded her that the church would be available for her and that they would keep her in prayer.

"Be blessed sister."

Jumping off the couch, Stephanie said, "Oh yeah, let me fetch my purse and pay you for my meal."

"That won't be necessary," Elder Brown assured her.

"Are you sure?"

The men nodded as they all headed to the door and Stephanie thanked them again, as her visitors left. Ten minutes after they left, Stephanie twisted her head toward the sound of banging on her door. She rushed to look out the peephole. The fisheye lens of the peephole exaggerated Donnie's head.

"Stephanie, don't make me break your door down. I will. Open this door now."

"Go away, Donnie. I'm calling the police. Please, leave my porch and property now."

"Open the door, Steph."

Donnie beat the door with his fist, hard and vicious. Suddenly, he started kicking the door, trying to break through.

Grabbing her phone, she dialed 911. "Please, help me, someone is trying to break into my house."

Donnie peered at her through the blinds while she was on the phone, and he rushed to his car and drove away.

"The person left," she told the operator.

"Can you identify the person's face? Was the person a man or woman? Did you recognize the perpetrator?" The operator asked with concern.

"Yes, I saw him. The man used to be my fiancé. He ran when I screamed through the door."

"What is his name?"

"Donnie Johnson. But Operator, he is a good person. He's just not taking the break-up well. I don't believe he will hurt me. He didn't break the door down; he didn't get into the house. He just knocked and beat on my front door. I called you all just to make sure he doesn't go off, on the deep end."

"An officer will arrive in two minutes."

Once the officers arrived, she explained the events of the day. She told the police about the report she filed earlier and they listened.

"Give us his address and we will speak to him. We will not arrest him because he didn't threaten you or force entry, but we want to talk to him to make sure that doesn't happen in the future."

"Thank you, Officers." She called out his address to them.

"Ms. Whitmore, your alarm work?"

"Yes, it does." Stephanie crossed her arms over her chest as if she suddenly got cold. "I didn't turn it on."

"Does he have the code?"

"No, he doesn't."

"Well, make sure you set the alarm in the future." The officer instructed and wrote something on his pad.

"I will. Again, thank you for coming."

They walked off the porch and got into their patrol car and left. Stephanie stood on the porch shivering. Finally, she turned, entered her home, and set her alarm. She became hungry and remembered the food the pastor and the elder brought. Going into the kitchen, Stephanie warmed up her meal, ate some, and then went to take a bath. Finally, her nerves settled, and she decided to go to bed to find peace. As she prepared to get into bed, her phone rang from a number that she didn't recognize.

"Hello?" Stephanie waited. The only sound softly vibrating through the phone line sounded like someone with labored breathing.

Finally, a more prominent voice stated, "You hit my man in the head with a fireplace poker. Watch your back." And then the phone went dead.

Chapter Five

For almost a month, Stephanie stayed away from Donnie. Now, more than a month later, Donnie still missed his fiancée. His broken heart reeled with pain because he lost her trying to play the field. He never thought his slickness would catch up with him, but he understood that what he did bordered on total stupidity. Why on earth would he bring another woman to his house with their wedding right around the corner? He tried to sow his oats before the wedding. When he thought about the truth of the matter, he loved Stephanie. Now, due to his libido and lack of restraint, he may have lost the only woman he loved. Ever since that messed up day, the woman he had been cheating with, Tabitha, had been relentlessly trying to force him to make a commitment to her. As a matter-of-fact, she rode his back constantly, wanting a monogamous relationship.

Her bedroom antics were superior, but he would never wife her. She was a barmaid he met while club-hopping with his friends. Not the kind of woman he would bring home to his mother. She didn't understand his culture, or his life, and did not fit in.

He wanted someone who was like his mother - somewhat in her image. Stephanie shared similar interests and reminded him of his mom. He let Stephanie slip away. He was going to fight to win her love. His life depended on it.

Donnie walked through the door of the Boys Club. He spent his extra time working with the young kids. He was trying to make a difference. He also understood the need to be different to make an impact on the children. He needed to practice doing better with his life decisions.

"Hey, Donnie." Little Kent called his name.

He knew that voice anywhere. He was assigned to mentor him over the past two years and could see a major difference in his attitude. His grades had improved. As a reward, Donnie and Kent attended Cardinals baseball games, movies, plays, and other simple things like dinners at restaurants and trips to the park and zoo. He loved supporting the kids whenever he could. He understood what they went through because he had experienced the same things.

"Donnie, man, what happened to your head?"

Jasper, an older kid, walked up, asking, "Dag, man, who busted a brother in the head? Tell me, 'cause me and my boys will handle them.

"What? So, you'll end up in juvenile detention? I can handle myself; you just continue to enjoy being a 13-year-old kid. You feel me?"

"Yeah, Dude."

"What I tell you about calling me and other adults dude?"

"I understand. I got this. Okay?"

"Make sure you do." Donnie gently touched him on the shoulder and looked into his eyes so he would understand he meant business.

"Okay. But who hit you?"

"That's grown folks' business."

"Okay. I was trying to help," Jasper said, as he looked down and his shoulders slumped.

"Thanks, Jasper, but I'm okay. I appreciate the love. Now, tell me what you have going on."

Suddenly, Jasper seemed tall again. He stood straight and smiled.

"Mr. Donnie," Kent leaned over toward Donnie. "...he likes this girl that comes here to the center. That's why he's trying to act all hard." Little Kent smiled. It was so contagious.

"Oh, really? He doesn't have time to think about girls. He needs to improve his grades. Right, Jasper?"

"Yes, sir," Jasper said, looking sheepishly.

"Mr. Donnie, what happened to your head?" Little Kent inquired.

"Son, I hurt it. Don't worry. I'm okay."

"I just don't know what I would do if something happened to you. I love you."

Donnie smiled. He loved Kent and all the boys he worked with, but Kent had his heart. He was seven years old and living with his granny. He was a very sad boy until Donnie started taking time with him. Now, he was a happy little boy who had friends and opportunities. No matter what Donnie did, he would always be in Kent's life. Donnie leaned over and hugged Kent.

"I love you too."

After he had helped the kids with their homework, they played a pickup game of basketball. He enjoyed his time with the boys. As he prepared to leave, he reminded the kids that he would pick both Jasper and Little Kent up at their house for the Cardinals baseball game. They were excited, both hugging him before running to get on the activity bus to go home.

Donnie patted his chest. "Lord, please help me get Stephanie back. My heart aches."

Chapter Six

*T*abitha Hassel's forehead dripped with sweat and her eyebrows furrowed. She was angry to the maximum, due to being ignored by her man. She spent the morning moping around. How could Donnie do what he did to her and act like he didn't care?

Ever since his so-called fiancée caught them, she hadn't heard one word from him. She called, but he never answered the phone. She texted, but he ignored her. Her insides boiled with heat and anger because she believed he used her. Being with Donnie ensured her the chance to come up, until that crazy, poker-swinging heifer walked into the bedroom. No way would this be the end for her and the extremely handsome money bags, Donnie Johnson. Nothing or no one would stop her from getting her man.

Tabitha grew up poor. Her mother, a single parent, who often left her with neighbors and friends so she could work as a stripper to feed both her and her young daughter, never married. Tabitha never met her dad. Her mother said she conceived her when she used liquor to give her the courage to dance and couldn't remember anything due to being extremely intoxicated. Some say that a child will become what they witness, and that is what Tabitha became - a barmaid and stripper.

She was doing okay, but now she accepted the fact that her beauty and her physique would change as she aged. Only 24 years old, her body already showed signs of aging. To offset not wanting to dance for a living, she decided to snag a well-off man to marry and take her out of poverty. But Stephanie Whitmore interrupted her goals. At least, that is what she believed. If Donnie wouldn't talk to her, she would make Stephanie suffer. Tabitha believed that if she continued to harass Stephanie with those phone calls, she would eventually let Donnie go for good. But first, she tried to call Donnie again. She went to her favorite's list on her phone, pressed his name, and his picture popped up.

He didn't answer his phone, as it went straight to voicemail. She decided to leave a message. "Hi, Donnie. I miss you and hope you are much better. It's been a month since I last saw you. Why don't you stop through tonight and the drinks and lap dance will be on me?"

Tabitha also typed the message from her phone as a text to Donnie. She would wait to hear from him, but if he didn't text or call her back, she would visit him at his home. As she reached to put her cellphone back into her purse, it vibrated.

Donnie: **Tabitha, I appreciate your offer, however, I am trying to work on getting my fiancée back. Take care.**

She typed, as she spoke each word from her mouth, seeming like cement, binding her thoughts into concrete words from her soul.

Tabitha: **"Oh, you're trying to play me like that? We will see, Mr. Sexy. I'm giving you a little time, but I won't wait for you too long."**

She waited... No response. Tabitha chewed on her bottom lip in great thought. "I'm not giving up. That's my ticket out." She said, loud enough for the other strippers to overhear.

****

It had been six weeks since Stephanie attacked her fiancé and dumped him. Although the ache in her heart grew stronger, she knew it was for the best. Her best friend, Regina, returned and helped Stephanie deal with her disappointment. Regina took her to church, dinner, and they stayed back and forth, at each other's place. Regina wanted to make sure Stephanie wouldn't run back into the arms of Donnie. After all, Regina didn't think Donnie served her friend well. He didn't meet Stephanie's standards.

Today was girls' day, and taking in a Cardinals baseball game would be a good distraction for her best friend. Stephanie took a three-month leave from her company, allowing her assistant director to handle her nonprofit organization. She needed the time to overcome her heartbreak. In addition, Elder Brown, Elder Duncan, and a Bible worker visited her weekly to have Bible study, which she enjoyed re-learning so much about God.

When Regina arrived to pick up her friend, she found her on her cellphone.

"I promise to visit your church soon. Your elders were very helpful. They frequently call to check on me, and I've completed four sessions with your team."

"I'm happy they've been helping you to study the Bible. Do you need anything else?"

"No, Pastor Winston. I'm fine," Stephanie said, as she waved Regina in and took a seat on the couch, playing with the nails on her left hand.

"What about the young man you were marrying? Is he okay?" Pastor Winston asked in a voice that became low and almost sensuous. His voice went down an octave, as he voiced his concern.

Standing up and grabbing her purse, Stephanie held up her finger to tell Regina she would be ready in a minute. "The last time I saw him, he seemed fine. I haven't spoken to him or seen him in over a month."

"Well, Sister Whitmore, I'm happy you are okay. I would like to offer a prayer for you; is that okay?"

"Sure, Pastor, I would appreciate that," she stated and then closed her eyes and bowed her head.

"Heavenly Father, I come to You in prayer, asking You to bless and protect Your daughter, Stephanie. You know her needs because it is You who's directing her life. I ask that You continue to guide and bless her and all those who are involved in this situation. Guide her steps, heal her heart, and be a presence in her life. I thank You for leading and watching over her. Continue to bless and keep her in

Jesus' holy and precious name. Amen."

When Pastor finished praying for her, she thanked him.

"I appreciate your prayer and kindness. Thank you, Pastor."

"You're welcome and please call us if you need anything. Also, the doors of our church are always open."

"Thank you and enjoy your day."

"You do the same."

Regina walked up on Stephanie, asking, "What's that all about?" She rolled her neck back and forth, demonstrating much attitude.

"He's the pastor I sought out when I caught Donnie in bed with that tramp."

"You realize I love you, right?"

Walking over to the couch to take a seat, Stephanie said, "Yeah, I realize. So, where are you going with this conversation?"

Following her friend to sit on the loveseat directly across from her, Regina reminded her. "Donnie's the one who made a promise to you. He asked you to marry him. When he asked you to be his wife, that meant he had put down the playboy status to be with only you. So, don't call the girl a tramp because she wasn't the one who broke your heart. He did that. She didn't ask you to marry her, he did."

"Okay, so I won't call her a tramp. But she's a whore."

"Okay, Stephanie. I'll give you that one. But remember, men make women promises, so don't be all mad at the woman. Maybe she didn't comprehend that fact. We tend to hate the women we caught the men with, but we should direct that anger toward the men."

"Well, maybe she didn't, but I kinda feel like she knew. My picture sat directly on the fireplace in plain view, as well as our engagement photo. I'll give her the benefit of doubt but that's it. And she called me and threatened me."

"What?" Regina stood up, alarmed. "You didn't mention that."

"Well, what would you call a woman - who now understands, even if she didn't know at first - that you were engaged, yet she still wants him and calls to threaten you about paying you back for hitting him in the head?"

Regina shook her head and sat back down to comprehend the ridiculousness, and to hide the laugh boiling way down deep inside her lower belly.

"Girl, please. Stop lying."

"Okay, her exact words were, 'You hit my man in the head with the fireplace poker. Watch your back.' Stephanie giggled so hard the tears hurried down her face. She reached up and wiped her tear-stained face. She was crying because the pain was now fresh again.

Regina jumped up from the loveseat and made a mad dash to her friend. She pulled her up from her seat and hugged her.

"My poor, dear friend, you didn't tell me you were dealing with a crazy person too. God bless you, girl. Now make sure you don't take her threats lightly. OK?"

"I won't," Stephanie said, as she embraced her friend and gently squeezed her back. She wiped her tears, assuring, "Time heals all wounds. I won't forget, but it won't hurt as bad."

"Yeah… right. Girl, let's get to this game before it ends. I got box seats too." Regina picked up her purse and grabbed her keys, as she strutted to the door.

"Wow, how did you get box seats?" Stephanie asked, as she followed her friend out the door.

Stephanie turned the alarm on and pulled the door closed, locking it.

"Don't worry about that. Let's just enjoy our day together. Finally, you're getting out of the house."

"Yeah, I've been stuck inside for a while. Thanks, sister, you're always here for me," Stephanie stated and then hugged Regina.

"Now, Steph, you're my girl, and you would do the same for me."

They both entered the car and Regina drove to the stadium.

Chapter Seven

*D*onnie picked up Kent and Jasper at the Boys Club, as promised, to take them to the baseball game. Both boys were so excited they could hardly contain themselves.

"When the game is over, we will go eat pizza," Donnie told the kids.

"Mr. Donnie, your bandage is gone from the top of your head. Does it still hurt?" Kent wanted to know.

"No, I'm good."

"Where is Stephanie? Did she hit you in the head?" Jasper laughed.

Donnie snickered. "Boy, you're funny."

"Then, where is she?" Kent frowned, reaching over and pulling Donnie's arm.

"We broke up, but I am trying to woo her back. I miss her."

"We hope she comes back. We love her too. Just like we love you." Kent smiled, and his eyes beamed like a lightbulb. "We can go back to her church and see her like we did last time."

Donnie reached up and rubbed Kent's head. "I love you and Jasper too. You both are some superb young men. But remember, we all went to my mom's church for friends' day. So Stephanie and I haven't been going to church anywhere regularly. Now, let's ride and make it to the game. Our seats are great."

"Thanks, Mr. Donnie. You always do things with us," Kent stated and then laid his head back into the plush, leather seats.

"Our mentor is the best ever. Everybody envies us." Kent said.

"The truth is, my little brothers are the best. I love you guys. Always believe that."

"Ok," the boys said in unison.

****

Donnie and the boys arrived at the baseball stadium and immediately went to the Cardinals club seats.

"Here are our seats." Donnie directed the boys to their area.

"Wow. Mr. Donnie, these seats are great. Thank you. The view is awesome." Jasper said as he clapped his hands in excitement.

"You can also order all the food you want to," Donnie said, as he continued to lead the boys to their seats.

Not long after sitting down, Kent jumped up and ran toward someone. Donnie got up to follow him.

"Kent, come back here."

As Donnie neared the person Kent ran to, he stopped in his tracks. There stood Stephanie, looking absolutely stunning. She took his breath away.

She stood there with Kent wrapped around her legs, squeezing her tightly.

"I miss you, Ms. Stephanie."

"Hi, Kent. I missed you too." Stephanie admitted.

She looked at Donnie and her heart melted. What she loved the most about her ex-fiancé was how much he loved helping kids. He would definitely make a great father. He gave his all to the kids he mentored. He wanted them to have a chance in life, secure, with a male figure who cared enough about young boys and men to help keep them alive. Too many mothers were losing their sons to graveyards and the streets. Donnie made a vow, a long time ago, to give back to the community which he'd followed through, to this day.

"Stephanie, I miss you. Are you okay?" Donnie couldn't help but admit.

"I'm fine." She ignored him but whispered into Kent's ear and told him she would visit him soon. She cuddled his little neck and kissed his chubby cheeks. He pivoted and ran back to his seat. Stephanie waved and blew a kiss at Jasper, who waited in his seat.

"Stephanie, we need to talk, please."

Donnie reached out to grab her hand, but she pulled it back before he touched her.

"Please, sweetheart. I'm going crazy without you. I love you so much. Please forgive me."

"It's too late for that. What's done is done. Our relationship is over. Please stop calling me. I will not give in."

Donnie took two steps forward, and Stephanie took two back.

"Hey, Donnie." Regina walked over. "This is not the place. People are looking. You and Stephanie need to handle this later and let the boys enjoy themselves."

Donnie ignored Regina. She never liked him anyway. He refused to listen to someone who tried to end his relationship with her innuendos. When he and Stephanie worked their situation out and became married, she would be the first person they would remove out of their lives. There would be no room for negative people in a new marriage.

"Stephanie," he called again, and looked at her with puppy dog eyes. His circular face and his eyes looked hopeful, yet sad. His brows furrowed, while sweat beads popped up on his forehead and began to travel down his face. He took out a small handkerchief and patted his face dry.

"Please talk to me. Just give me a chance. I messed up."

"We'll talk later, okay?" She told him anything to stop the conversation. She needed to move away from him. She was willing to forgive him, but she would never forget. She also internalized she could never trust him. "Call me later," she said to get away without an argument. Stephanie told him this before she walked back to her seat with Regina.

"Please answer the phone," Donnie pleaded.

Stephanie shook her head to indicate okay.

"I'll call you." Donnie said winking his right eye.

"Thank you, Stephanie, Donnie said eagerly, and then walked to his seat looking a little hopeful.

Regina took Stephanie's hand and led her back to her seat.

"The nerve of him. You better not stoop low and go back to him. Once a cheat, always one. I don't want you hurt again."

Regina said as she leaned closer to Stephanie.

"I know. In Bible study, we are taught to forgive. I've done that. I'm glad he is still mentoring his boys. They need him. Honestly, he's a good person."

Regina rolled her eyes and added, "Just not for you. Let it go."

Stephanie peeped over to the right side of her seat and observed Donnie watching her. He winked his eye. She turned her head and remained focused on the game. It was hard to concentrate on the game with Donnie so near. She still had feelings for him, even if she did deny that openly. It would be stupid to think her heart would fail her. How could she fall so quickly out of love with a man she wanted to spend the rest of her life with? But the truth was staring her – literally - directly in the face. He couldn't be faithful to her.

She was confident, in her heart, after watching him in the bedroom with that woman. What they were doing, and the grunts and moans she heard, was not just sex; he was making love to her. 'The truth will always set you free' is what her mom always told her, that's why she prayed to God, asking Him to heal her broken spirit. Deep down, she truly believed that if Donnie was really the man God had chosen for her, he would never have allowed himself to break such an important vow when he told her he was faithful, loved only her, and asked her to be his wife.

Thinking about that beautiful day and her happiness brought a sudden tsunami of tears to her eyes. She couldn't control her emotions, as they flowed so quickly down her face. It was as if a huge floodgate suddenly opened and water flowed over the sea level, causing significant, economic damage. But this wasn't colossal for others, only her, and the damage was far from being rebuilt. After all, if she returned to him, every step outside her peripheral view would lead her to accuse him of philandering. As a matter-of-fact, she refused to be that woman with knowledge of her husband's cheating, yet continued to make love to him, risking themselves to all kinds of diseases and illnesses. All she could think about lately was seeing his sexual organ swinging from left to right after she hit him in the head and he jumped up and tried to run after her. So no, this was a man who was risking his health for pleasure and there was no way she would ever trust him again.

"Stephanie, do you want to leave?" Regina handed her dearest friend a tissue and gently caressed her left thigh.

Wiping her tears with the tissue, she blew her nose and said, "If I get up, he will know I am still hurting. I don't want him to notice my pain."

"Sweetheart, a blind man can see your pain. I wouldn't be angry if we left."

"No, just give me a moment and I will be okay."

Thirty minutes later, Stephanie asked Regina to leave with her. It hurt immensely to watch him, but to view him as he kept turning, flashing, and winking his eye at her, was just too much too soon. The women grabbed their personal belongings and walked out. When Stephanie turned to give Donnie one last look, she met six sad eyes staring at her. She waved to the two beautiful boys who had stolen her heart when Donnie first started mentoring them. She hoped they would continue to be okay because Donnie had never disappointed them like he did her. She was certain he loved his mentees. Stephanie waved because she would never see them again. All of them waved back.

Chapter Eight

"*H*ello, Sister Green. This is Sister Clay. How are you today?"

"I'm doing great. How are you?" she asked, on the other end of the phone.

"I will be better once you clear something up for me."

"How can I help you, Sister Clay?"

"Well, I'm looking for a church home. The last one I attended, the pastor had sex with folks in his congregation."

Sister Green took a deep breath and inhaled to show her agitation.

"That's not the information I received. My acquaintances attend that church, and we were told the pastor married the lady people accused him of having premarital sex with."

"I don't care what someone communicated to you. The pastor, and that gal, sinned by having sex and married to cover up their sin."

"Well, that's not my business, yours, or anyone else's. Nobody's but God."

Smacking her lips to show her frustration, Sister Clay said, "Before I attend another church filled with sinful and gossiping people, I'll stay at home."

"Well, the first way to make sure you are not in a gossiping church is not to participate in confusion yourself."

Sister Clay held the phone. She wanted to chew Sister Green's head off but decided to act more civil. She didn't have a relationship with anyone in the church, so she didn't want to start trouble.

"OK. You're right. We must be careful how we present ourselves. Someday, I will tell you what happened to me at my former church."

"Talk to God. He will hear your cries and keep them close to His heart. He will do for you what no other person can. I would stay in prayer. By the way, you're welcome to attend Bible study and new membership classes as you await the baptismal. Try to meet the people in the church before jumping in with your eyes closed. All things are not what they seem, and all people are not who they say they are. Stuff like that happens in every church. But people come to church to feed their souls. They come to learn about God and to congregate with people who are trying to accomplish the same thing. Gossiping and backstabbing is not healthy, and that crap is like bringing heavy baggage to break down the carousel of love."

Sister Clay smacked her lips and mimicked how Sister Green talked. "Mmm hum. That's right." She giggled.

Sister Green heard Sister Clay laughing and making fun of her. She decided to ignore her actions.

"Everyone may not get to salvation at the same time, but they are in service to try to make it eventually. Remember, people come to church to seek salvation and to change their sinful ways. They don't need any stumbling blocks in their way. As a member, I will not be a stumbling block for another Christian or a person seeking God. I'm about to hang up, so nice talking to you. I'll speak to you at Bible study. Goodbye, Sister Clay."

Sister Clay hung the phone up, walked into her kitchen, took a glass out of the cabinet, and grabbed a bottle of gin. She poured some into the wine glass, took a sip of the strong liquor and shook her head.

"Now that shocks the throat going down."

That didn't go the way I wanted the conversation to go, Sister Clay thought to herself, subconsciously rubbing her throat as the gin began to slowly work its magic. *Mama always said, 'kill them fools with kindness first.' I'll be kinder and not so transparent, but I'm going to work on getting the information I need. I swear something ain't right with Pastor Winston. Why would he allow a woman to come to his church with blood on her hands? That woman killed somebody, and I am going to find out who she killed. This time, I am going to show God I am a true Christian who cares about the people who become members. I am a good person. Nobody puts me out of their church as if all's okay. I am fighting back.*

"I need your help, God, to expose these fake preachers."

Sister Clay decided to go to her room, change clothes, and make some more phone calls. She made her next call to Trisha.

Trisha Coates was a former member of a group folks once referred to as the Piss Patrol. They were a group of young women who didn't complete high school and others considered uneducated, ghetto-fabulous troublemakers who threatened, bullied, and fought people in their neighborhood. Once, Pastor Davis of the True Church, in which Sister Clay held a membership with, met and recruited them to attend Bible class. Trisha fell in love with him and wanted to fight anyone she perceived as a threat in getting close to him. Young, with a bad attitude and a negative perspective, she once considered his wife an adversary, but Denise Reese ended up marrying the good preacher. She and Trisha became friends after Denise observed her shopping in a department store and approached her in a friendly way.

Unfortunately, Trisha started off in the church under the influence of Sister Clay. Although now baptized, she occasionally talked to her old friend.

Trisha loved being a Christian. Once she gave her life to God, so many positive things happened. She passed her classes and received her General Education Diploma. She enrolled in community college and worked part-time on campus. Plus, she loved working in the church and expressed her happiness. At last, Trisha met a wonderful, Christian man and her life changed for the better.

Trisha believed that if she changed, anybody could. She didn't fear having a relationship with Sister Clay because she wanted her to accept God as her Savior, and felt that all gossiping and drama that preceded her friend would end.

"Trisha, what you been up to, sweetheart?"

"I'm doing well," she answered and shared all the things going on in her life. She was so proud of her accomplishments.

"Girl, you just be extra careful because you are not in the clear. Becoming a better and more informed person will take years to wipe the ghetto out of you. I mean, you've laid in the dump with fleas for so long, it's going to take more than attending a fake church to be clean."

Trisha took a deep breath and counted to 20 backwards. She wouldn't allow anyone to rain on her parade. Trisha loved that God cleaned her up and she refused to allow anyone to pull her back to the gutter attitude and life she once lived.

"Okay, Sister Clay, you witnessed where I came from, but God made many promises to us. You don't understand my story, so you cannot see my glory. My Bible says God is not a liar and I believe the Word. So, I may not be as clean right now as God is going to make me, but you can be sure He has wiped my slate clean with His mercy and forgiveness."

"That's all I am trying to do... remind you that you came from the gutter, and with those gutter attitudes, it's going to take time to develop new ways. You're rushing into this new life and what is going to happen is this: the faster you rise, the worse your fall. Don't try to act all high and mighty all of a sudden. The same folks you rolled in the hay with as a sinner are the same ones you'll end right back up with if you lose sight."

"Sister Clay, I remember where I came from. But this is the difference, I didn't have a relationship with God but I do now. I am a new creature in spirit and in God. I have a past, but my experiences will help me to try to help others change their lives to a more positive one."

"Girl, skip out of the way with that stupid stuff. You can barely read."

"Father in Heaven, I need You to intercede for me. My friend is in need of a spiritual makeover," Trisha prayed aloud.

Suddenly, Trisha heard several loud thuds and jerked the phone away from her ear to prevent damage to her eardrum.

Sister Clay had taken her phone and hit the desk three times. It seemed she was trying to knock something off or out of it. She rotated her eyes to the top of her head and shook her head from side-to-side, as if she was trying to clear the equipment. Then, just as quickly, she put the phone back to her ear.

"No you didn't just start praying for me. I don't allow anyone to do that without permission. You are not skilled enough, not spiritually inclined, and darn sho' not experienced enough to call God on me. Listen, girl, you don't know me well. Let me ask you this: do you understand who I am?"

"I guess not," Trisha responded with a slight pause, then she spoke again. "I want you to remember something the pastor said last week. He read this from Proverbs 16:18, which said, 'Pride goeth before destruction and an haughty spirit before a fall.' I took this to mean that a person who is high-minded and thinks they are better than others and believes they are superior, will suffer a huge fall from grace. You be careful how you treat people. I used to be a gossiper, fighter, and a person who never sought anything but fun. But I'm changed. God saw fit through Pastor Davis to invite me to his church and help encourage me through Bible study. Like he helped me, I want to help you."

"I got one thing to say to you, little girl. Don't mention Pastor Davis and his sinful self to me. There is nothing that sex addict can teach me. You all are the fools who allowed him back into the pulpit. I am not stupid, and I am not a fool. No man in the role of a pastor should ever exhibit that behavior with a whore. You all act like he is God."

"Wait one second. The problem is that many people like you acted like Pastor Davis is God. Like he was perfect and could do no wrong. But he is a man, imperfect, yet striving to do God's will. God is the one who is perfect, and God is the person you should be trying to please."

"Girl, shut the hell up. I will call you later. You're talking like a fool. Someone must be sitting by you 'cause you're acting high and mighty. Who's the dummy sitting next to you? Oh, you don't have to tell me. I will find out. But listen to my words; I love you enough to help you see things my way and I will."

"I'll be praying for you. You be good though, Sister Clay."

Before Trisha uttered another word, the phone she held went dead. She turned the phone around to be sure, and just as she thought, the minute counter on her cellphone stopped.

Thinking about that weird phone call made her think about Pastor Davis's beautiful wife, Denise. She would call her soon to receive some of her special, positive energy and to pray with her. She refused to allow Sister Clay to push her back into being her old self. She didn't like that other person she displayed then, and she certainly didn't like her now.

Chapter Nine

*B*ored and feeling lonely, Stephanie laid on the couch and glared at the television. She wasn't into the program, a show she had never seen. The TV was watching her. Her cellphone rang. After three hours of silence, the sudden sound scared her.

She was still being texted by Tabitha. That girl was seriously a nutcase to think Stephanie had hindered her love life. When she texted Tabitha back, she threatened to show the text messages to the authorities if she sent one more. As a result, she had not heard from the love-sick girl for the last 24 hours. Stephanie sat up and reached for her cellphone on the coffee table. She slid the screen to the side and answered.

"Hello."

"Hi?"

"Is this Stephanie Whitmore?"

"Yes," Stephanie answered and then sat up straight, looking at her left hand tapping her leg. She guessed who was on the phone.

"Hi, Sister Whitmore. I was wondering how things are going with you."

"Pastor Winston, how are you?"

"I'm doing great. I spoke to the elders who are working with you and they said you are a very quick study and had plenty of questions. They tried to answer them all. But if you need me to work with you—"

Stephanie stood quickly to her feet, cutting him off. "No, Pastor, I'm fine. The elders are doing a great job with helping me find scriptures and sharing additional resources and information."

Both Stephanie and the pastor held the phone for a half of a minute, but the stale air lingered a bit too long. Then he said, "I would like come to visit you. Would that be okay?"

Suddenly, she started walking and pivoting pacing the same path in her carpet. She was a little nervous. Why did the pastor want to talk to her? *What were his intentions?* She wondered.

"I think that would be fine."

"When would you be available? Is today good? I am free today without any appointments left, so this would be a good time. I'll bring us some dinner. Would that be okay?"

Stephanie laughed. "Yes, today will be fine."

The pastor didn't want to spend too much time discussing menus, so he suggested pasta, vegetables, and a dinner salad. Stephanie agreed.

Although Pastor Winston was excited to see her again, he understood that she was still too hurt to think about another relationship. Even though that was the case, he couldn't keep her off his mind. Ever since the day she ran into the church looking for help, he had thought about her. Once they touched, a spark of electricity so powerful shot in his arm and shocked him. The force jolted him backwards. When he looked into her eyes, he recognized that she had experienced the same thing. Although she jumped, her soft, brownish, teary eyes tenderly lit up with a flash of fear.

****

Stephanie walked through her house to make sure everything was clean. She loved to show off her home and didn't mind keeping things tidy and smelling like fresh flowers. She had one hour to find some fresh-cut flowers and come back. Stephanie passed the hallway mirror and stared at her reflection. For the first time in two months, a little happiness tried to seep into her soul. She grabbed her purse, keys, and set the alarm before going to buy flowers.

Silently, she asked God to bless her. *Dear God, please mend my broken spirit. There are days where I hurt so bad, and the betrayal is still so strong, but I pray to God as instructed in Matthew 7:7, 'Ask, and it shall be given,' so I'm asking you, Lord, to lighten my heart, eliminate my pain, and fix my broken spirit.*

****

Arriving home in the nick of time, Stephanie had only a few minutes to put the flowers in water and into a vase. Then, she rushed into her room and quickly showered and put on a black, maxi, sleeveless dress, with her flat, black, beaded sandals. She spun around to check how she looked in the long mirror. Refreshed and cute, she brushed her hair out. Just as she was putting the brush back into its holder, her bell buzzed. She peered at the clock on the dresser and saw that it was 5:30 p.m. He was prompt. He told her he would be there at 5:30 and he was true to his word.

Stephanie barely had 15 minutes to prepare when she returned from getting the flowers. She was impressed. Stephanie felt this meant he was a promise keeper, in some way. She liked that if he said he was going to do something, he did it.

Stepping to the door, without knowing the agenda, Stephanie reeked of confidence.

Ever since the day in his office, Pastor Winston, through the church staff, had made sure a sense of peace surrounded her. He was gentle and polite but decisive. She didn't think he would ever do anything he didn't want to do. A man of his word equated a reliable, confident Christian man. That was alright with her. She didn't need to pretend or be fake around this pastor. He seemed like a good person.

She pulled the door open and met the face of one of the sexiest men she had seen since, well, Donnie. His body released the most sensual scent as the air pushed into her door. If there had been mistletoe, due to the holiday season coming upon them, she wouldn't have resisted giving him the biggest kiss ever. *Were preachers supposed to be this fine?* She thought, shaking her head and then smiled.

When the door opened, Pastor Winston looked at the beautiful, modelesque woman in front of him. Stephanie's facial structure looked like God had created her features to look like no one else's... just for him to enjoy. Gorgeous wouldn't adequately define her beauty. He felt stuck to the floor. It seemed like they were in a solid stance, staring at each other and wondering who would win. Finally, the pastor spoke.

"Hello, Sister. It's good to see you. May I come in?"

Stephanie reached up and finger-combed her hair.

"Sorry, Pastor, I lost track of myself for a minute. Come right in."

She moved over and widened the door. As he passed her, she smelled the food he carried in a large plastic bag.

"The kitchen is that way." She pointed for him to head to the right and she followed. She didn't realize just how hungry she was. Since the breakup, she found herself eating less and dropping unneeded pounds.

He placed the food on the counter and asked, "Where's your bathroom? I need to wash my hands."

"Follow me." She led him to the guest bathroom located down the long hallway, and swiftly turned around and went back to the kitchen.

He whispered to himself, "My God, she is so beautiful. Thank You for making us in Your image, Lord." He smiled as he whispered again, "Thank You, God."

Stephanie fixed their plates and poured two glasses of tea. She figured he didn't drink sodas or high-calorie juices; he was too fine to be a junk food junkie in her opinion. She had made some pre-sweetened tea and set water on the table for each of them. When she looked up and saw him walking towards her, the spark that had ignited within her in his office returned. She gave him the once-over. The pastor had smooth, pecan-colored skin, beautiful, sparkling, white teeth, a slim waist, but was muscular and a buff, sharp dresser. His hair was cut in a low fade, and he was at least six feet tall. She thought, *where do they find preachers who look like this? His wife must be proud to cradle her arms around him.* "Please, sit down." Stephanie instructed and then followed suit and sat across from him.

"Sister, would you mind if I offered a prayer?"

"That would be great, Pastor."

"Lord, thank You for this food we are about to eat for the nutrition of our bodies and thank You, Lord, for good friends. Bless Sister Whitmore and myself, as well as our families. In Jesus' name. Amen."

Putting a forkful of pasta in his mouth, he asked, "How long has it been since you've been absent from church?"

She picked up her drink and swallowed some tea before responding. "About three years, give or take visiting with my mom or attending a wedding."

"Well, I'm happy you are returning, right?"

"Better late than never." She smiled, as she picked up her fork and scooped up some pasta and vegetables.

"This pasta and vegetables are good. Thank you so much for bringing dinner."

"No problem. Now, tell me what do you do for a living?"

Laughing nervously, she said, "Do you really want me to answer that?"

"Is it bad?"

"Maybe to you." She smiled.

"Yes, please tell me."

"I own a nonprofit company, and I am an author."

"Wonderful. I have not read any of your work."

"Do you read drama or erotic fiction?" Stephanie tried to gauge his reaction, but he kept his face neutral. She continued, "...and I do write some Christian drama."

"Not quite... I mean, I don't read that kind of stuff."

"But there is nothing wrong with writing it, right?"

"Well, God did give us talents and He wants us to use them. There is erotica in the Bible."

"Yes, indeed."

"But I believe God wants us to use those talents to glorify Him, to teach people about His love and about love period. There is nothing wrong with using your talents. God gave them to us, but I believe He wants us to glorify Him in all we do. So, if erotica takes the reader's mind off of Him it could cause some people to sin, which is what God hates, that's a problem. In the Bible, He teaches us that it is wrong to lust or to covet another man's wife or a woman's husband."

He looked at Stephanie and noticed that she had a perplexed look on her face.

"In essence, if someone is reading your books and the stories cause the reader to lust after the characters or even others, it might be a problem. If it causes readers to seek porn and become addicted, it might be a problem. Now, if you write erotica and the message is that it's wrong to lust or seek love from someone else's spouse, I can see that might be okay."

"I can see that. The story should focus on a strong message for the reader and how the reader uses the information," Stephanie acknowledged and then tossed her hair back with a gentle shake of her head.

Her eyes twinkled, and the confused look on her face vanished.

"That makes a difference." She smiled.

She had been studying the Bible and trying to learn what God expected of her and how He wanted her to use her talents. Though she was good at writing erotica, sometimes she felt it was not in the best interest of the reader. She wanted them to grow and to find strength in a stronger message.

"Maybe, I'll write erotica for married couples."

"Use your talents, Stephanie, and pray. God will lead you in the direction He planned for you to go." He looked at her and smiled.

Pastor Winston did not want her to think he was criticizing or putting her talents down. He clarified, "I think writing is wonderful. To be an author is impressive. You can write stories and visit all the places you want. You can take the readers anywhere in the world. That's a blessing. I'm interested in reading your Christian work."

"Thank you so much, Pastor. I feel so much better."

She reached for her tea and took a swallow. When she sat the goblet on the table, she placed it a little too hard, and the bottom hit the walnut and glass table making a banging sound.

"You okay?" he asked, thinking he may have angered her, which is why her glass hit the table so hard.

"Yes. The glass slipped from my hand. But you've given me much to pray about. I appreciate this conversation very much and I'm so happy you came by." Her smile was genuine. She let out the breath she held while waiting on his opinion. It felt good to talk about her feelings about her writings.

He took another forkful of pasta, looked up at her, and winked his eye as he chewed his food. "This food is very good, or maybe I was starving."

"It is very good." She stirred her pasta, as she prepared to spoon more up on her fork. She took a mouthful before she reached for additional sauce.

As the pastor continued eating, he explained how he had wanted to see how she was doing. "My elders are working with you, and I do try to get updates, but I wanted to talk specifically to you to assure you were okay, considering what you have been through."

"I'm doing fine. I'm no longer engaged. Donnie is giving me my space. Even though he wants us to reconcile, I'm not interested."

"How can you be so sure? Are you still praying about it?"

"I asked for strength through prayer to follow the steps God is ordering for me. I believe He has something greater for me to do. I think God is working on me."

"Tell me, why do you think God is working on you?"

"Well, Pastor, I suffered from the entire situation. I don't ever remember hurting so badly. God directed me to your church, and I met you and your elders, and now I'm in a home Bible study class. When I started dating Donnie, I stopped attending and have been absent from church too long. I wasn't able to convince him to go to church with me either."

"You're right. I believe He is steering your life. Sometimes, God will orchestrate things to happen to make you take notice or do what He planned for you. He directs our paths since He is the one who already planned what we are going to do anyway."

"Yes, God understands our needs. Sometimes I wonder why we end up in situations that hurt us when He can stop us from doing things not good for us. I grew up in church. It's easy to start going and hard to return once you leave.

Shifting in his seat, Pastor Winston put his fork down, which made a clicking sound when it hit the plate, and then put his hands together as if in prayer.

"Life is about free will, Stephanie. God loves us so much, He gives us a choice to follow Him. He doesn't demand us. He doesn't want to force people to believe or follow Him."

"I just don't get that. If He made us and designed our every move, then He already worked out who is going to follow Him. So why all this studying and trying to encourage us to do something when He already knows who is going to Heaven?"

"Stephanie, God gives us a choice to live with Him or without Him. It's like with anything we must deal with in life. For example, we live in a world where there are rules and regulations we must follow. If we run a red light, we may be ticketed, or hit another car, injuring the driver. But we had free will to stop or go. Either way, whatever you choose to do, there are consequences; whether they are positive or negative, there are still consequences."

Pastor Winston reached for his tea. The ice had started to melt. When he reached for the glass, the ice tossed around as he drank the tea. Stephanie took the pitcher and poured more tea into his glass.

"Thank you," he stated.

Smiling like she won the lottery, she replied, "You're welcome."

"So, Stephanie, free will is the choice to choose your consequences. Even though God knew what we would choose before we were ever born."

"This is what bothers me. If I have free will to decide to go to Heaven or Hell, and I choose to go to Hell, while God has predestined me to Heaven, how is that free will?" she asked, rubbing her forehead. The lines creased in her forehead and Stephanie looked even more confused.

"The thing is, you have free will to either reject Him or to accept His saving grace. Whatever you choose, He knew you would choose it, He planned it, He purposed it, He desired it, and He predestined it."

The pastor knew he needed to spend more time on this subject with her but decided to end the conversation and give her some Bible verses to read.

"The fact is, God loves us and wants us to be with Him, but He doesn't want to force anyone to be with Him. That's not what He wants, so He gives us the free will to decide."

"I kinda get it."

"This is truly a great discussion. I want you to fully understand it. I'll give you more information to study on this topic, and I will discuss this on next Wednesday at Bible study. I know you have Bible study at home with our elders and Bible workers, but would you come to the session at church?"

"Yes, I will attend."

"Great. I think it would be very helpful."

They continued to eat in silence. Suddenly, the shrill of Stephanie's phone sounded in the house. It was so loud it was as if the tone bounced from the wall to the ceiling. The noise scared her, and she jumped. Stephanie laughed when she realized it was the phone.

"You okay?"

"Yes," she said, as she slid the bar over on her phone to talk.

"Hello?" she answered, as she pushed her chair from the table, causing the legs to drag angrily across the wooden floor. Getting out of the chair to find privacy, she said, "excuse me," and walked into the living room.

"I'm busy Donnie? I know I told you to call me. But what do you want?"

"You know darn well what I want. I want you to stop this silly mess and come back to me. I was wrong. I apologized. What more do you want?"

"Your apology is accepted. I want you to leave me alone. I will never trust you again. That's not a good relationship to have with someone you are supposed to love."

"Stephanie, every relationship has problems. We learn and grow from them. I'm on my way over."

"No. Don't come over here. I don't want you near me."

"You act like you're scared of me. I will never hurt you."

"You already have. Don't you dare come this way. I will call the police."

She didn't realize she'd raised her voice several octaves. When she turned around to walk into the kitchen area, Pastor Winston was standing in the doorway with a concerned stare on his face.

"Are you okay?"

"I'm sorry. I'm fine." She assured as she passed him and asked, "Are you finished with your dinner?"

"Yes. Thank you."

He picked up his plate and glass and strolled to the kitchen sink. Stephanie took the utensils out of his hand and put them into the sink.

"I appreciate dinner and your company. I enjoyed myself. Thank you for the Bible study."

He moved to the table and grabbed the paper he had written on and handed it to her.

"Here are the Bible verses I wrote down for you to read. After you study these, write down any questions, and we will address each of them next week. Is that okay with you?"

"Yes. Thank you."

"Well, thank you for having me over. I have to leave. I look forward to seeing you at Bible study," he stated and then walked toward the door. At the door, he reached out to shake Stephanie's hand and a bolt of electricity shot from his hand to hers.

Dropping the paper, she jumped and shrieked, "That one hurt."

"I'm so sorry." He took her hand, and they both bent down to look at her hand to make sure nothing happened. When they did, their heads slammed into each other. Both of them clutched their foreheads and tried to rub the pain away.

"Wow. You okay?" she asked.

"Yes. I better leave before we hurt each other." He laughed. She giggled.

"Bye," they both said at the same time. Stephanie watched until he entered his car and drove off.

Sauntering to the living room and sitting on the couch, Stephanie said aloud, "Lord, keep that pastor away from me. I don't want to fall for a married man."

Her phone rang and she answered, "Hello?"

"I told you to leave Donnie alone, but women like you think fat meat ain't greasy, so it seems like I'm going to have to show you it is."

"I've asked you not to call me anymore. I guess I'll have to report you to the police."

"You don't scare me. Call them. I'm thinking, if I don't beat your butt first, I'll press charges on you for swinging the poker stick at me. After all, you did hit me."

"I didn't hit you, but I should have."

"I saw Donnie on your street. Let me catch you with him again and see what happens."

"Girl, go somewhere with your childish self. If that man wanted your stale self, he would be calling you, not me, and you wouldn't be harassing me."

"That's it. Your ass is grass."

Stephanie laughed as she slid the bar on her phone to off. "So sad," she said out loud. "He gave me up for trash." She took her remote and flipped through her television channels. Rearing back into the couch, she closed her eyes and thought about the fine man she had dinner with a few minutes earlier.

"Lord, help me. He is so good-looking and compassionate."

Chapter Ten

"You did what? Are you crazy?" Elder Brown paced the floor in the pastor's study. "You are going to lose your ministry. What is on your mind?"

"I don't see anything wrong with me having dinner with her," Pastor Winston said before he pulled his chair out from the table and sat down. "I'm interested in her."

"Pastor, you can't be going over potential members' homes and sitting across the table eating with them," Elder Brown advised. He waved his hands in the air, demonstrating his frustration with the pastor.

"Are you telling me this woman has made such an impact on you that you're willing to lose everything?" He rushed over toward the pastor and stood over him while he pressed his palmed hands into the conference table. "Did you go over to her house as the pastor of this church or as a potential suitor?"

"I went as the pastor," he answered and drummed his fingers on the large, chestnut conference table. "I took her dinner." He closed his eyes and considered whether he believed he went only as the pastor. He had to admit to himself that he had feelings for her.

"Don't do that again. You are putting this entire ministry in jeopardy. What if she tells someone you are harassing her?"

"Why would she do that?"

"Because she sought you out for help, not to sleep with. As a pastor, you cannot just show up at single women's homes, take them dinner and not think they are getting a message you are interested in more than having a pastor and member relationship. You cannot send out the wrong signal."

"But I can send out the right one...I'm interested in her. I like her as a man likes a woman. She's not married."

"Because you are so attracted to her, you are not thinking right. Your actions are dangerous, and you must be careful. You may lose too much, so play this smart. If you are, indeed, interested in this lady, we will continue to invite her to church. Meet her on sacred land; work with her on activities in a group. This way, you two can experience friendship with each other outside of you counseling her. Right now, she is in counsel with the elders and though we give updates, you may be confusing sympathy with romance."

"I'm not confused, but you're right. I've been praying for someone to love. I believe she is the person God sent me. I feel it so deep in my heart, but I'm not doing this right. I'm not officially counseling her, but I feel I am."

"Well, if you experience that so deeply, then we'll flesh-sit you."

"You will what?"

The pastor stood up and stuck his hands into his pants pockets. He looked at Elder Brown like he had lost his mind. His eyebrows furrowed, which looked like a zigzagged tic tac toe.

"What do you mean by that? I am not a child."

"No one is saying you are. Flesh-sitting is like babysitting the flesh. When you are around her, we will help you stay focused."

"So, you think I cannot preach and enjoy a woman's company without someone monitoring me?"

"Pastor, you could lose so much if this gets out of hand." Elder Brown looked flustered. His face had turned red, his cheeks became dark, and his eyes sunk in. He continued, "I mean no harm. I'm only trying to help, which is what I am supposed to do."

Pushing his chair under the conference table, Pastor Winston marched over to Elder Brown, and with their faces almost touching, Pastor Winston said, "I think I can handle my personal life without you flesh-sitting me." He pivoted around and headed toward the door. Then, he quickly spun around. "Thank you for looking out for me. I'll think about what you said. Flesh-sitting the pastor. What in the world are you thinking?" Pastor Winston shook his head and grabbed the door knob, jerked the door open, and slammed it on his way out.

Elder Brown pulled a chair from under the table, took his Bible and opened it.

"Lord, guide me on this one. The pastor is sprung."

He turned the pages of the Bible. "Lord, help me find something to help the pastor."

The pages of the Bible started flipping over. When they stopped, it landed on Proverbs 18:22 which read: "Whoso findeth a wife findeth a good thing, and obtaineth favour of the LORD."

"Lord, are you trying to tell me this is the pastor's future wife? If so, we will protect and help him to do this the way you want it to be done. This happened unexpectedly. He's been lonely, but I guess stuff like this is true. Love comes when you least expect it. Help us, Lord, to handle this according to Your will."

Elder Brown stood up and closed his Bible. He strutted to the door and reached up, turning the light off. As he locked the church up, he smiled thinking about the pastor's face when he told him they would babysit his flesh. *You could've bought him for a dollar,* he thought, as he walked toward the parking lot to his car with a smile on his face and a chuckle in his heart. He took his phone out of his pocket and called the pastor.

When the pastor said hello, he said, "Pastor, I'm trying my best to protect you and the church. As the head elder, it is my charge. I'm sorry how I responded to your feelings. I am trying to do my job, which is to guard the spiritual life of the flock. It is my duty to serve as a peacemaker, prayer warrior, and teacher, as well as to be a leader. So, I want to make sure the decisions you make are not just based on emotion, but spirituality. I'm sorry if I offended you."

"I appreciate your service to the church, the members and me, but I am a man and I can handle my personal affairs. I'll make sure the lines don't cross. Thank you for your concern."

A pause settled on the line, and for a half a minute, no one said a word. The pastor broke the silence.

"I appreciate your call. I'll speak with you later."

"Ok. Thank you."

They both ended the call.

Chaoter Eleven

"**W**hat are you doing here?"

Donnie stood up from behind his desk and hurried to the front of it. Aggravated, he stated, "How dare you show up to my place of employment."

"You wouldn't respond to any of my calls," Tabitha said, as she stood there in all her sexiness, looking stunning. Her tight, pencil skirt and white, collared shirt with the buttons open showed her perky breasts. Her red lipstick emphasized her big, puffy lips. Her voice sounded soft and sweet. Donnie didn't want to be angry at her, but showing up on his job did not sit well with him.

"Didn't I tell you I would contact you?" he asked seriously, as he stood right in front of her. The lines in his forehead were prominent and large, green veins poked through his creamy, light skin, pronouncing his anger.

"This is inappropriate. Whatever you need to say, do it outside of my place of business."

"We need to talk about what happened. I love you and I need answers." Tabitha stood with her feet planted firmly on the floor. She had no plans to move or leave the room until the matter resolved or some action netted her man back in her arms.

"Apparently, you don't grasp what I'm explaining. There is no you and me. I am in love with Stephanie. Nothing or no one will stop me from reuniting with her. You were just something to do for the moment." He strutted over to her and grabbed her arm. "Leave now, or I will call security to escort you out. Please don't ever show your face at my job again."

"You think it's going to be that easy to send me away after feeding me all those lies to accomplish that you wanted to lay with me? Did you believe you were going to hit it and run? Not here. You and I are not over. Not by a long shot." Reaching up, she yanked his shirt collar and snatched him closer to her. Donnie wiped the speckle of saliva that landed on his face from her warm breath blowing on his face as she spoke.

"You didn't handle me as well as you thought. I am not to be played with."

Donnie forced her hands away from his clothing and spoke with gritted teeth, "You will never touch me like that again. Leave my office now."

Tabitha pivoted and walked toward the door. "This is not over, Donnie. I love you." She quickly exited his office.

Donnie went back to his desk and picked up the phone to talk to his secretary. "Don't you ever allow anyone to walk into my office unannounced."

"I'm sorry, sir, but I went to the bathroom and—"

"I don't care if you were hanging off the roof; make sure that desk is covered when you leave it." He banged the receiver down and dropped into his dark brown, leather chair and relaxed his head back. "These women are crazy. Got to be more careful," he acknowledged loudly.

He picked up the phone and dialed Stephanie's number and waited until her voice message stopped. "Stephanie, call me, please. This game is over. We need to talk. I love you, and I'm ready for you to come back to me." Reaching up to rub the stress from his temple, he called on God.

"I need you, Lord. I want Stephanie back."

****

Tabitha sat in her 2003 Ford Explorer in the parking lot of Donnie's job crying. She wiped the tears trailing down her face and vowed to snatch her man back from Stephanie's paws.

Deep down, she thought being with him gave her a good chance at a better life. She had struggled for so long and was tired of living paycheck to paycheck. She was sick and tired of the men who came to the bar and expected her to allow their dirty, filthy hands to roam her body. She wanted her life to improve, but not at the cost of her dignity. In her mind, she believed Donnie loved her. *If only that woman never entered the picture,* she thought.

Tabitha had no intentions of returning to the double-wide trailer her mom lived in with her flavor of the day. Her mother changed men like most people switched shoes. With every change, since the age of 12, she had to fight off dirty, old men. The last time, she hit one in the head with an iron skillet and promised him the next time he put his dirty hands on her, she would chop them off. He ran from the house like he had robbed the mob and they were hot on his trail. This angered her mother, who threw her out of the house until the school counselor reported her to Human Services Department for Families. Since that time, Tabitha and her mother, Mary, never got along.

She refused to give up on Donnie and run home with her tail tucked between her legs. She had more tricks to play before she gave up. She started up her SUV and waited until it stopped the loud roar it gave off as a result of the truck's age and pulled off the lot.

Tabitha picked up the phone and called her archenemy. When she recognized her voice, her blood boiled.

"You ruined my life and you are going to pay for it," she threatened. Hearing Stephanie's voice made her angrier. "I hate you," she admitted.

"Okay, Lady. I understand you are hurt...I am too. But you need to target your anger to yourself. You knew Donnie and I were together. Our pictures were all over the house. My presence stood out clearly. You ignored it. You're suffering because you chose to be with a man whom you knew to be engaged. Be angry because you couldn't make him love you. I had nothing to do with it. If you call me again, I promise I will report you. I haven't done it yet because, like me, I knew you were hurting. But you are directing your anger at the wrong one."

"I hate you," Tabitha screamed into her phone, right before she ended the call.

Chapter Twelve

*S*tephanie was preparing for the Metropolitan Ministerial Alliance for Ministers meeting for the current month. They were a group of ministers who met monthly to address many issues that affected members and pastors. The team promoted unity among pastors, churches, and local leaders. They also provided information and resources to people in their churches, as well as in their community. The ministers worked to solve problems and to encourage pastors to remain faithful to God and their ministry. Stephanie decided to host the group, as many nonprofits did, because they helped those in need. She decided to ask Pastor Winston to come to the meeting since she did not observe his name on the roster.

Stephanie picked up the phone and dialed his number. He answered on the second ring.

"Hi, Pastor Winston. This is Stephanie Whitmore."

"Hi, Sister Whitmore." The pastor held up his finger and excused himself out of the meeting he was in. "How are you?"

"I'm fine. What about yourself?" She experienced clumsiness and took a seat in her office chair to become more comfortable.

"All is well. What can I do for you?"

"Have you heard of the Metropolitan Ministerial Alliance for Ministers?"

"Yes, I have."

"Well, they are going to meet at my office, and I wondered if you wanted to attend. There will be an opportunity to meet some of the other pastors in your conference, and your wife can join in some of the ladies' activities. I didn't see your name on the ministers' membership rosters."

"I would love to attend. I'm sure my wife would like to meet other women, if I had one." He gave a hearty laugh. "I'm not married."

Stephanie held the phone and tried to wipe the smile that was expanding across her face. Wow, she didn't expect him to say that.

"I'm sorry, Pastor. I assumed you were married."

"I hope to be someday." He chuckled.

Stephanie took a deep breath that sounded across the phone lines. "I don't know what to say." She lost her voice. She couldn't think straight. She realized that she had been hosting a single man in her home. Though she wanted to look presentable in his presence, it never occurred to her to ask about his marital status. She had to pray and ask God to help her because he mesmerized her with his cologne.

"Well, the meeting is scheduled for this coming Monday. If you send me your bio, I will introduce you to the group. I'll also send you the meeting information."

"Great. Give me your email address and I will email it to you."

She gave him the address and then stated, "If you have any questions, don't hesitate to call me back."

"No problem. Thank you so much for inviting me."

"You're welcome, and I'll talk to you soon."

They both hung the phone up. Stephanie could barely wipe the smile off her face. It had been three months since she and Donnie had broken up. She didn't want to be sad anymore. But this time she promised herself to wait on God. That is why she continued the Bible classes. She wanted to make sure the next man in her life would be a Christian.

****

Stephanie met Regina for dinner. They decided to go to O'Charley's Restaurant. She dressed in a white summer dress with ruffles around the bottom and wore her silver sandals. She stared at herself in the mirror and then spun around. The vibes floating in the air surrounded her in beauty.

Once she arrived at the restaurant, the hostess took her to her friend.

"Hey, girl. Long time no see," Stephanie said, as she wrapped her arms around her friend and kissed her on the cheek.

"Stephanie, the big case I'm working on is draining. I cannot wait until it's over. The case is taking up a lot of time."

"The murder case of those rich folks out in Ladue?"

"Yeah. The suspects are blaming each other. But we plan to prosecute both to the fullest extent of the law. That robbery went wrong," Regina said as she looked over the menu.

"I think I'm going to order the Santa Fe Tilapia."

"I'm going to request the Bayou Shrimp Pasta." They both gave their orders to the waitress.

"Girl, what's been going on with you?"

"Well, I had dinner with Pastor Winston." Stephanie put her elbows on the table and leaned forward with a huge smile on her face.

"What? You act like you're in love. Tell me, are you?" Regina inquired, as she picked up her margarita and took a sip. "Mmmm... this is so good."

"No, I'm not in love, but he is so attractive. He's just trying to help me."

"Or is he trying to help himself to a cutie?" Regina chuckled and picked up her glass and sipped again.

"Honestly, he's not like that. He's a good man. You should hear him pray."

"Just be careful. You've already suffered one heartbreak. You don't need any more pain. Isn't he married anyway?"

The waitress brought their salads. "Thank you," Regina said.

"He's not married, which shocked me. I never pegged him as single."

"Maybe he is gay," Regina surmised, taking a mouthful of salad, as she laughed. "Too many of these men are in the closet."

Picking up her wine, Stephanie took a drink before answering.

"No. Not gay. There is no way. There are no signs."

"Most of the time there aren't. Just keep your eyes open and your heart safe. But I am glad you are venturing out. Being with you allows me to witness your healing. Good for you... Thanks," Regina said to the waitress as she placed their plates on the table.

"What about you? When are you going to find a man, and settle down?" Stephanie asked, as she twisted her pasta around her fork and took a big mouthful.

"Well, I'm too busy now, but when I secure a break, it's on."

They both laughed and continued to talk about so many things. They agreed to try to visit each other often and to stay updated on each other's lives. Just as they paid their bill, a young blond, Caucasian woman passed them and purposely dropped a glass of strawberry soda on Stephanie.

"I'm so sorry," she said, with a smug face.

Stephanie screamed and stood up. "You ruined my dress."

"You ruined my life, skank," Tabitha hollered back.

Stephanie rushed up and tried to grab the woman but Regina pulled her back.

"Fighting her is not worth it, Stephanie. Don't go down to her level."

"I'm not finished with you," Tabitha warned with a smirk, as she walked out of the door.

Stephanie stood there shaking. Her hands trembled. Sweat beads popped out all over her body and tears lingered in the corners of her eyes.

Chapter Thirteen

"Hello, Donnie?"

"Hey, Stephanie." He sat down in his chair and took a pencil and started doodling 'Donnie loves Stephanie,' then he drew a heart around his words.

"Please call your hound dog off me. I'm going to have her arrested for harassment. I'm filing charges today. I don't believe the charges will stick because harassment is so hard to prove, but at least I need to make the police department aware of Tabitha and her games."

"What are you talking about?"

She screamed at the top of her lungs, "Your girlfriend tossed her drink on me today at O'Charley's Restaurant and promised me that's only the beginning. I'm so angry." Stephanie started crying.

Donnie pulled the phone back to prevent his eardrum from bursting. "I'm sorry, Steph."

"I'm so tired of being Ms. Nice. Stop her, Donnie, or something bad is going to happen."

"I'll talk to her, baby, but we need to talk. I miss you so much. Did you have enough time to think? I want you back. I love you," he pled as he caressed his forehead.

"The relationship is over. I'm not interested. One day we can be civil to each other, but I could never trust you if I came back. That is no way to live. Besides, this Tabitha has drawn the wedge even deeper. She keeps calling me and making threats. With all this, I can never come back."

"Let me deal with her." he said.

"How are your boys doing?" She calmed down and twirled her hair around her finger.

"They are fine. The boys keep asking about you. They want to spend time with you. Just come and share some time with us."

"Donnie, tell them I said hello. I need to go. But handle your girl or things are going to become ugly."

Stephanie ended the call. She sunk back into her couch and tried to relax her mind. She wanted to think of something pleasant to stop her from becoming angry again. She decided to go visit her parents.

****

Several hours later, Stephanie arrived at her parents' house. She pulled into the driveway, taking a deep breath. The long drive helped her relax. Her parents lived in O'Fallon, Illinois - about 45 minutes away - on a good day. Using her key, she let herself in.

"Mom, where are you?"

Mrs. Joan Whitmore strutted into the living room in a beautiful, royal blue, summer, maxi dress.

"Oh, shucky shucky. You look fantastic, Mom."

Joan spun around and modeled her dress as the hem swished around her ankles. "This is how you keep your man on his toes."

Without warning, Stephanie started sobbing and collapsed on the couch in the family's living room.

"Oh, baby, I'm sorry. I forgot you were going through so much. You've been doing so well." Joan sat down next to her daughter and massaged her hands.

"It still hurts." She laid her head on her mother's shoulder.

"Being apart is going to hurt awhile. Breaking up with someone you love is a painful, hurtful experience. But like I told you, it is better you found out about Donnie before you married him. If you hadn't, it would be harder to sever ties."

"I realize that. I'm glad I found out too. But it still doesn't stop the pain."

"I've been praying for you. Remember what I said. Allow God to lead you. Pray and ask Him to help you find the right one, He will." Joan shook her head and stroked her daughter's hair behind her ear. She continued, "You couldn't drag that boy into church when you met him; you stopped coming." She shook her head. "Ump, ump, ump. I tell you young women, you lose them where you found them, if you don't allow God to lead you. If you find a man in the church, your chances are better."

"Mom, there are some roguish, so-called Christians out here. Besides, he went to church with his mom and took me on several occasions."

"A few times is not enough, now here you are hurting, but remember, the Bible says in Matthew 7:20: 'Wherefore by their fruits ye shall know them.' You understand that?"

"Yes, Mom. You recognize Christians or non-Christians, but sometimes, you think you can change the person you love."

"By your actions you might be able to change them. But most times in relationships, the wrong party usually changes the Christian if they are not strong enough in their faith."

Stephanie reached into her purse and pulled out some tissue. She wiped her tears away and blew her nose.

"I let Donnie change me. But I'm back in Bible study."

"That's beautiful." Joan hugged her daughter. "Maybe you can visit us over here more, too."

"I will, Mom. Where is Dad?"

"He'll be home shortly." They sat on the couch and talked for several hours.

Hours later, her dad, Ben, finally arrived. Ben smiled and opened his arms wide for his daughter to come to him for a hug. It had been a while since they had been in each other's presence. He kissed her on her cheek several times and co-signed with his wife about relationships and allowing God to guide her in finding the right person.

Joan, Ben, and Stephanie decided to eat some cake and ice cream. Joan prepared three bowls and gave everyone a slice of carrot cake.

Stephanie's resolve to survive her pain became stronger when she left her parents' house. It was as if a light bulb had turned on in her head. All her life, her mother told her 'when you learn about God's Word and study the Bible, when you need God's Words the most, you'll remember.'

Stephanie drove the 40 miles back home in deep thought. Feeling much happier, she would continue the Bible classes. Thinking about God and His goodness brought a sense of comfort to her and made her life feel renewed. It would take time for the pain to go away, but she believed with God, she would come out on the winning side.

Chapter Fourteen

*M*onday morning, Stephanie led the ministers who had arrived into her large conference room. She had set up a continental breakfast for their nourishment. She went into her office to grab her notepad and ink pen, and to remind her secretary about her schedule, as she headed into the meeting. When she turned around to walk into the room, she bumped into Pastor Winston.

"We are going to have to stop meeting like this."

He interrupted, "Shocking each other and slamming our heads together." They both laughed, thinking about the other times they had bumped into each other. He reached out to shake her hand. "Nice seeing you again. Thank you for inviting me."

"You're welcome. When I didn't notice your name, I thought it might be something you would be interested in. I'm just the hostess for this month. Next month, another agency similar to ours will do the hosting."

"I visited your website and saw how much work you do for the community. I'm very proud of your contributions."

Stephanie started blushing and her cheeks shined like they were covered in cherry-colored blush. She had flushed and turned red. She noticed the pastor's smile extended across his face and all she could do was watch as he showed his beautiful, white, straight teeth. She decided to show him around and then took him into the meeting that was about to start.

Pastor Jules Jayson led the meeting. After introductions, had been made, they went straight to the agenda. They had one person who had asked for a personal meeting. After they had cleared the agenda, they asked Sister Clarice Clay to come into the meeting.

She walked into the meeting and sat in the chair. Sister Clay wore a gray, long sleeve suit with a black shirt underneath. She had on black gloves and a black and gray hat. She turned her head around and searched the room.

"Well, I came in today to ask for your assistance. But I realize you all will not be able to help me."

"Why is that, Sister Clay?" Pastor Jayson asked, as he leaned forward to make her stay comfortable.

"The person I am here to complain about is right here. It is Pastor James Davis."

"Pastor Davis, would you mind stepping out? We will inform you of what is happening after we meet with Sister Clay."

"No problem. I'll be in the waiting room." He took his Bible, notepad and left the room.

"Well, he threw me out of his church because I didn't like the fact that he slept with a whore before he married her."

"How did you confirm they had sex? Were you there?"

"No, I didn't have to be in the same room or bed to realize you don't have to lay down with fleas to bite someone."

"What?" One of the other ministers uttered.

"Do you realize you are spreading rumors you cannot substantiate?"

"I'm telling you the truth. That woman is trash. I saw her leave his house one morning. Next thing, they were in Vegas galloping around in the hotel I stayed in."

"They were on their honeymoon."

"Pastor, now we all understand how folks cover up their sin. People think they are hiding their sin, but there are those Christians

- like me - who are watching. The Bible says watch while you pray, and that's what I'm doing."

"Sister, I believe the Bible is making reference for each of us to watch and pray that ye enter not into temptation. That means you and me watching our behavior. We are not to spread rumors about people."

"This is not a rumor. I peeked that woman leaving his house in the wee hours of the morning. Now, Pastor, you realize that ain't right. Then they throw me out of church because they sinned." She tossed her Bible on the conference table, smoothed out her shirt, and crossed her legs.

"This committee doesn't deal with rumors or innuendos. Do you have a complaint?"

"Yes. I do. I just set the scene." She turned her head around so she could look directly into the eyes of each minister. She needed to see their facial expressions to determine if they were going to support her. "I want to know, can I worship at that church? Do the pastor and members have a right to ban me from services?"

"As you may have researched, Sister Clay, state and religion are separated. Therefore, you can be barred from a church the same as you can be barred from someone's home. You see, a church is not required by law to be open to all the world and its people. The amendment precludes any law that would enforce people to have the right to embark on a private place."

"Pastor, I'm not sure what you are saying. I didn't do any research, for your information."

"Well, to make it clear, churches can limit your attendance or have attendance for those who remain in good standing. Whether one is in good standing is a rule of the church and not a law. So, a person can be removed or banned from any place if they are found to be disruptive, offensive, lewd, or dangerous."

Reaching up and slamming the table with her fist, she looked around as the pastors at the table jumped at the sound her hand made when it slammed against the wood.

"That doesn't make any sense. The church is a public institution." Sister Clay screamed and stood up to make her presence and anger duly noted.

"It is important that you understand this. The land where the building sits is considered public. Church grounds are private property. The grounds belong to the church. Churches can stop you from coming on their property and to their church. If you're asked not to come back, and you do, you can be arrested."

"So, you are saying I can be thrown out of a church?"

Pastor Jayson opened his Bible, bent down his head, and whispered a prayer to help him explain this to Sister Clay. "The rules of the church can set laws, ethics, and the congregation is off limits to the law. The ethics are governed by the church and its own higher authorities."

"So, to make the story short, they can ban me?" She pulled her chair up close and sat down.

"Yes, you can be banned. Because a church rule is not the rule of law."

"No, no, I will not accept that." Sister Clay shook her head from side-to-side. Tears pooled in the corners of her eyes and began to spill down her cheeks.

"Did Pastor Davis ask you to leave?"

"No, the board suggested it."

"Then I would say, if you love the church and can be ministered under the current pastor, meet with the board and tell them you want to return. The pastor seems reasonable. If you can follow the rules of the church and not cause harm or danger to anyone, maybe they will reconsider their decision."

"No. No. I will not grace that church with my presence again. If I'm not wanted, I will stay away. But they will pay," she threatened and jumped out of her seat, causing Pastor Jayson to quickly rear back out of her way. The other pastors stared with shock expressions on their faces.

"What do you mean they will pay?"

"Why nothing, Pastor. I made a statement out of anger. Thank you for your time." It was as if another person had come into the room. Her anger reformed, she faked a smile, and her voice appeared softer and sweet. Sister Clay picked up her purse, her Bible, shook her head, and pivoted to leave. She smirked and parted her lips and began to sing, "The devil is a liar and a conqueror too. He don't mind how to conquer you. If I could, I surely would. I'll stand on the rock." When she said the rock, she slammed her foot down as if she'd killed a bug. Then she turned, giggled, and left.

"I have never," Pastor Jayson said.

Suddenly, the door swung open and Sister Clay stuck her head in the door, flicked out her tongue, and sang off key, "and you never will." She slammed the door.

The ministers all turned and looked at each other. They had never dealt with an experience like this one before. So, they called Pastor Davis back in and discussed it with him. He explained he'd not thrown her out and that the day they announced their marriage and re-baptismal was the last time they had seen Sister Clay. The pastors gave him some advice, and they all huddled together and prayed for Pastor Davis, Sister Clay, the Alliance, and their churches. They all voted to allow Pastor Davis to utilize their attorney, if needed.

As the pastors departed, they all recited Philippians 4:8 and 9: "Finally, brethren, whatsoever things are true, whatsoever things are honest, whatsoever things are just, whatsoever things are pure, whatsoever things are lovely, whatsoever things are of good report; if there be any virtue, and if there be any praise, think on these things. Those things, which ye have both learned, and received, and heard, and seen in me, do: and the God of peace shall be with you."

Chapter Fifteen

tephanie waited on Pastor Winston to complete his conversation with the ministers. She asked her secretary to bring him to her office when he was ready. Her phone rang as soon as she hung up from her secretary, Mimi. "Hi, this is Stephanie."

"What are you doing, little girl?" Regina laughed. "Is that man on your property?"

"What man?" Stephanie grinned and drew circles on her notepad.

"Don't be acting brand new because Pastor Winston is on set. So, what's up?" Regina murmured, "Boom, boom, boom."

"Sister, what's that supposed to mean?"

"Dramatics, girl. I want to know what's up."

Stephanie muttered, "He is here for the meeting. Girl, I need God. Either he is fine or I'm still suffering from the concussion I gave Donnie three months ago."

"Now that is silly. You didn't get hit; Donnie did. Since he did what he did, as long as the pastor is single, go for it."

"Not preacher girl material. I cuss, drink, swear at drivers when I get angry and cry when I'm mad sometimes. This sister is too moody, too sexy, too smart, and too intelligent to get mixed up with a man who has to cater to a lot of crazy, emotional women, and he doesn't need another person like me. Plus, I write erotica."

Giggling, Regina said, "You so silly, and you are supposed to be educated. You are so ghetto-acting. I'm going to have you relocated."

"You remember what I told you about that ghetto mess, baby. Not me, no how, no way."

"Girl, call me tonight. My meeting is about to start. Don't forget; I want to scrutinize everything about you and cutie. You didn't invite him to that meeting for others to look at."

"No, seriously. I want Pastor Winston to join this ministerial alliance. They help folks in need of help, spiritual prayer, and jobs. These ministers are serious about God's work."

"Okay, girl. I realize they are. I just think you and the pastor have feelings you are not acknowledging, and trust, it's alright to have feelings because he is a man and you are a woman. Go for what you want."

"I'll call you tonight. Mimi is bringing him to my office now. Bye."

"Call me tonight."

"Okay."

****

"Ms. Stephanie, I brought Pastor Winston back to speak with you." Mimi guided the pastor to a seat at the small conference table in the office and offered him a chair. "Do you want anything to drink? Coffee, water or a soda?"

"Water would be okay. Thank you." He unbuttoned his jacket and took a seat.

Stephanie sauntered over and asked, "Do you think the alliance could be beneficial for you?" She took a seat across from the pastor and crossed her legs.

Just then, Mimi trotted into the office and handed the preacher a bottle of water and a napkin. "Thank you," he smiled at her, and then turned his attention back to Stephanie.

Pastor Winston looked at Stephanie's legs and then back up to her eyes. "Thank you so much for inviting me. Several pastors briefed me on the group, and I had several invitations but hadn't taken the time to attend a meeting. I do feel they could be extremely beneficial in assisting all our ministries." He beamed. "I was a little shocked about Sister Clay and her complaint, but I thought Pastor Jayson handled it well."

"Yes, he did. I think having the support of other pastors and being able to hear what is happening is so helpful, and can serve as guidance to all of you. That is why I wanted you to join. You assisted me and I just wanted to return the courtesy."

"Well, you didn't have to do that. But thank you. How are you, by the way?"

"I'm fine. God has blessed me."

"Stephanie, would you like to have lunch today?"

"I'm sorry, Pastor, I can't. I have another meeting to attend."

"I'm sorry. I didn't mean to be so forward." Pastor Winston stood up to leave. He extended his hand to Stephanie. "Thank you for inviting me to the meeting. I appreciate it."

"Pastor, I am available for dinner. Would you like to come by and I'll prepare us something?"

His smile radiated. "I would love to."

"What about six p.m.? I'll prepare salmon, salad, and vegetables. Is that okay?"

"I love salmon." He grinned. "I'll be there with bells on."

They both giggled. Stephanie walked him to the door and thanked him.

"I'll see you later."

Pastor Winston shook Stephanie's hand and left the office. As Stephanie headed to her office, Mimi asked, "Boss, is he married?"

"No, Mimi. He's not." Stephanie shook her head. "Never would I want to deal with a pastor and drama." When she sat at her desk her mind wandered, and she asked out loud, "If I don't want to deal with drama, why am I smiling and inviting a single preacher to my house?" She bowed her head. "Guide me, Lord. I don't want to get hurt again. I'm letting You take the lead. Would You, Lord, take the lead in my life?"

When Stephanie raised her head, there was peace.

Chapter Sixteen

*D*onnie decided to do something special for his boys. He hadn't seen them in a while and was concerned about what they were up to. He contacted the Boys Club and inquired about his little brothers. He was unable to reach them at their home addresses. Donnie was informed that Jasper was in detention for stealing and Kent was in a temporary foster home because his granny was in the hospital. Donnie asked and received information to contact the social services department handling the placement. He was given permission to have contact with Kent. Donnie also requested information to become qualified to be a foster parent.

Donnie contacted Kent's foster mom, Terri Morgan, and asked if he could pick the child up for an outing. With the support of Kent's case worker, he was granted the right, especially since he had already been through the background checks and fingerprinting.

He arrived at Ms. Terri Morgan's home to pick up Kent and decided to take him to a movie and to Dave & Buster's. The place served excellent food, and the kids loved their game room. He wanted to have a nice, laid-back day and forget about all the problems he was experiencing.

Donnie couldn't understand, for the life of him, why he couldn't let Stephanie go. After all, it was he who strayed on her. To be honest, he had been dipping and dabbing into other women since he met Stephanie, but he had fallen hard for her. Why couldn't he be faithful to a woman he loved? As he marinated on that, Kent asked,

"Where is Jasper? He usually comes with us."

"Jasper is in juvenile detention. You know what that is?"

"No. What is it? Is he okay?"

"For now, he is fine. Juvenile detention is a place they send kids who are disobedient, who steal and don't follow the rules. Jasper took something that didn't belong to him. You cannot go around taking from people. Do you understand that?"

"Yes. My granny said stealing is wrong and says there's nothing more she hates than a thief. She said if you lie you will steal."

"Your granny is right. Stealing is wrong."

"Granny also said God cannot stand a thief. It's one of the Ten Commandments."

"Your granny is right. You should not bear false witness against your neighbor. To do so is lying."

"Donnie, why don't you go to church?

"I don't know. I went when I was young, but I stopped."

Kent turned toward his big brother, touched his leg and said, "Maybe if you go to church, Stephanie will come back to us. I miss her so much."

"So do I."

"Why don't we surprise her and go to her church." Kent clapped his hands, like he just came up with a very good idea, and his eyes were beaming with excitement.

Kent glanced at him and smiled. He loved seeing Kent smile and showing so much happiness. It made him happy seeing the child happy. "Remember what I told you? Stephanie and I were not attending church. We went to my mom's church."

"Well, invite her to your mom's church..." Kent said as his smile faded.

"Let's enjoy Dave & Buster's and we'll see Stephanie later. Okay? Donnie said while tilting the boys head and tickling his nose. That made the child giggle. They entered the car and Donnie put the key in the ignition.

I cannot wait until we get to Dave & Buster's. I'm gone beat you in the games too. Just wait." Kent said, while bouncing in his seat and laughing.

"Okay. We'll see Stephanie later. The glow in his eyes dimmed. His eyelids hovered over his eyes like a window shade.

Donnie reached up and rubbed Kent's head. "You're such a great kid. I love you."

Kent's eyes began to shine again. His lips slipped into a half-moon smile. "I love you too," Kent said, as he turned the radio up a little louder.

Chapter Seventeen

*S*tephanie was nervous. She wanted to date again but wasn't quite ready. God had sent her to that church to save her life, not to become attracted to the pastor. She was so mixed up. She liked him and found him attractive, but she was uneasy due to the fact that it was wrong to have those thoughts about a man who was in a leadership position for God.

As she prepared the table, the doorbell buzzed. She passed her full-sized mirror in the hallway and checked out her appearance. Stephanie was wearing a black, asymmetrical, rouched, mesh dress that captured every single curve of her body. The skirt of the dress draped around her waistline, and the shoulders were wide, exposing her smooth skin. The dress was sexy and Stephanie looked stunning.

She strutted to the door in her 'Cammie' pointy toe pumps with the ankle caged in. When she reached the door, she took a huge breath to gain her composure. She was nervous. Never had she experienced the kind of nervous energy her body was emitting. She was in her home, entertaining again, after losing a man she thought she would be with forever. Shaking her head to rid herself of the past pain, she opened the door.

A smile spread across her face like a river that over-flooded from too much rain. When she looked at him, he was taking her in from head to toe. He stepped into the hallway of her home and reached out, pulling her close to him in a hug. His embrace gave her a sense that being in his arms was right. He whispered, "You look fabulous."

"Thank you. You're looking all handsome yourself." Boundaries had now been established. This was clearly a date with two people who were interested in each other. This was not Bible study.

Stephanie led Pastor Winston to the living room. "Please, have a seat, Pastor." She swung her hand around the room, letting him know he was free to sit anywhere.

Pastor Winston pulled his black pants up and sat down on the couch. "Do you mind if I call you Stephanie?"

"No, please do." She sat across from him.

"In that case, please, call me Daniel." He chuckled. His smile was beautiful. His lips were so kissable. She crossed her legs to gain control of her raging hormones. He was so handsome. He wore a black suit with a white polo shirt trimmed in black inside his jacket. They did a lot of small talk about the meeting with the clergy, and then he stood up and removed his jacket.

Daniel was so fine, and his muscles were pronounced through his shirt. He prepared to lay his coat on the couch. When he turned to drape it on the back, Stephanie found she could not take her eyes off his butt, which looked like a beautifully-shaped muscle.

"What did you think about the clergy meeting?" Stephanie asked, attempting to get her mind back in a safe space.

"I thought it went very well. I like the goals and purpose, and how the ministers are helping the congregations and others."

"What about Ms. Clay?" Stephanie leaned forward. She didn't want to miss one word. She thought about her past encounters with this woman. The first one happened years ago, and it was not good.

She first met her at a local store. Ms. Clay bumped into her and would not say excuse me. When Stephanie said it for her, Ms. Clay asked management to call the police and have Stephanie arrested. The store management ignored Ms. Clay.

"That was something. She seemed overly concerned about a married couple. God brought the two together. I am friends with James and Denise, and they are Christians. The Bible says, 'You will know them by their fruit.' Now, I do believe that if they were fornicating before they became married, then they have asked for and received forgiveness. However, that is between them and God. Sister Clay doesn't have anything to do with that. My understanding is that they both were baptized again and asked to be forgiven. So to keep bringing it up, and looking for trouble, that's a problem." Pastor Winston shook his head to demonstrate his frustration.

"It's sad when church members fight or try to harm each other." Stephanie said as she crossed her legs and leaned back into the couch.

"I know. Sister Clay is adamant about persecuting them but that is for God. I pray she doesn't lose her soul trying to take someone else's. The truth is… too many people are like Sister Clay. Their focus is always on others and what sin they are doing. They fail to check for their faults or even admit they have them. But I do like the way the committee handled the situation by voting to allow Pastor Davis to stick with his agenda with Sister Clay and to use their attorney. They did a great job." Pastor Winston eyes followed Stephanie as he completed his statement.

Stephanie stood up.

Looking at Stephanie to get a clue about what she was about to do, Daniel said, "I'm not sure the results or the decisions helped Sister Clay, but they won't be able to help everyone."

"Right, Pastor. I almost forgot you were here for dinner. You must be starving."

"Daniel." He smiled, and Stephanie placed her hand across her heart. That smile would be the death of her.

"May I use your bathroom to freshen up?" Pastor asked with his smile lingering across his face.

"Sorry, Daniel. You remember where it is?"

"Yes, I do."

She pivoted and walked to the kitchen area. Before the pastor moved, he stood in the same spot staring at her. Stephanie was a beauty and that dress made him pray.

"Lord, help me. That dress, that body," he said. Finally, he moved and went to freshen up for dinner.

At dinner, they discussed everything. It was so easy to talk to each other. They had so much in common. Often, they found they did many of the same things, like counseling, finding resources for people in need, sharing information and uplifting folks who were feeling down. They laughed a lot and enjoyed the meal Stephanie had prepared. As the evening settled down, the pastor remembered he left something in the car. He excused himself, after helping to clear away the dinner plates and cleaning the kitchen together.

"I'll be right back." He strutted to his car. Stephanie told him to leave the door open so he could walk right back in. He walked out smiling.

While Stephanie was putting the rest of the dishes up, Donnie walked into the house. "Stephanie," he called.

She walked into the living room and stopped in her tracks, dropping the glass she was holding. It bounced but didn't break.

"What do you want?"

Donnie walked closer to her. "I want you back."

"Please leave, I have company. Please. I don't want to have you arrested."

"I saw him. I just need you to know I still love you. I was with Kent and he misses you."

"I'm sorry Kent misses me, but I am not his parent. You need to leave now." Stephanie looked over her shoulder and saw the pastor coming back. She started shaking. "Please, Donnie. I have company. Just leave. No trouble, please."

"Is everything okay, Stephanie?" The pastor walked in and stood close to Donnie. He laid the flowers he went to get out of his car on the table in the hallway. "Is there a problem here?" The pastor's appearance became harder. He was not afraid.

"I'm leaving. Stephanie, I'll call you. Please answer the phone." Donnie backed out and asked, "Would you at least speak to Kent? He's in the car."

Tears rushed down her checks. "That's not fair. Don't force him into this, Donnie. That's wrong. He's a child. Don't play with his heart. He needs to forget me."

"He wanted to see you."

"Please, let it go and leave. Tell him I was not home, and please, do not come back or bring him here."

"She asked you to leave." Pastor moved closer to him.

"I'm leaving, dude. Stephanie, are you sure you want this to be over?" He looked at her with big, sad, puppy dog eyes.

"Yes. It is over."

"I'm so sorry. I hurt you bad. Please forgive me." With that, Donnie turned and walked out the door.

"Are you okay, Stephanie?" I didn't want to cause a scene. I saw the young boy in the car when I was walking back to the door.

Daniel moved toward her and put his arms around her. "Are you ready to start another relationship? I mean, is this over? You may still need time to heal."

"Yes, it is over, Daniel." She moved herself out of the pastor's arms and walked toward the door to lock it. She touched the flowers and picked them up, sniffing them. "They smell so good, and they are beautiful. Thank you."

"They are as beautiful as you are. He walked over and planted a soft kiss on her lips. Stephanie responded. Daniel needed to kiss her again, and he did. She accepted his lips again.

"I want to see you again. I enjoyed being with you. Would you go out again and again with me?"

"Are you asking me for a date or a relationship?" She looked into his eyes with a little hesitation.

"I'm asking for dates that could blossom into something more." He took her by the right hand and lifted it to his mouth, kissing her hand. "I want to make sure you are ready."

"Thank you. I would love to go out with you."

They walked to the door and kissed again. "Lock the door. I will call to let you know I made it home."

"Okay," Stephanie responded. When he walked out the door, she watched until he backed out of the driveway. Then she laid her back against the door and touched her lips. She connected with him. She enjoyed the kiss and couldn't wait to feel her lips against his again.

Chapter Eighteen

*T*abitha sat on the steps of her trailer and wondered what her next move would be. She was so broken. How could a woman fall so hard for a man? The truth was that she knew about Stephanie. She saw her photos in the house and even found her clothing there when she was sneaking and peeking for evidence of another woman. She regretted not being direct with Donnie about him having another woman because now she was the one hurting and plotting her next move.

Now, she knew how it felt to be the other woman in a relationship. Tabitha had secretly been having sex with Donnie for over three months. She believed she could change him and make him want her more than he did Stephanie. She did whatever he wanted her to do in bed because she wanted to please him. She had even tried a threesome with him, inviting a stripper into bed with the man she loved.

Tabitha needed Donnie to believe in her and to understand his importance to her. She would do anything for him. He still wanted her… She hated her… She hated the woman her man could not forget. She wanted her dead. Although she had never been violent before, something about loving Donnie brought the worst out of her.

As she sat on the raggedy, loose, wooden steps, she plotted her next move. She refused to go back to being poor, little, ugly Tabitha. She could almost hear the kids from her school days taunting her. "Little, nasty Tabitha, got no clothes, got no shoes, got no booty, just ugly and muggy. Who's gonna love the ugly, dirty girl?"

She spent many days and nights crying. Her mother did nothing because she was too busy drinking and trying to find the next man to pay her bills. Tabitha refused to be like her mother. Donnie was her improvement. He was the one who believed in her and promised to take her to the next level. She didn't think loving him would leave her sitting on the same kind of rotten steps she sat on when she was a child, begging for love. Who was going to love ugly Tabitha now?

Her phone rang, and she hit send and answered it. It was an old friend who was a known crackhead. She had a little job for him. She didn't want to hurt anyone, but she wanted to scare them. She told Jimmy, the crackhead, exactly what she wanted him to do. She would give him 200 dollars once she found out the job was successful.

****

Stephanie exited her car and was walking in the parking garage of her building. She had arrived to work 15 minutes earlier. It was quiet because she was an early bird and there were only two cars parked in the garage. As she walked, the only sound was the clicking of her red pumps across the concrete.

She thought she heard a noise and stopped and searched around for where the sound was coming from. Hearing nothing else, she proceeded to walk. Suddenly, a hand covered her mouth, and the man whispered, "I should rape your lovely self, but I only want your money. Give me all you have." His breath was putrid. It reeked of funk, like he had been eating babies' boo boo. He was breathing on her neck, and his crusty lips touched her skin, scratching her. She almost threw up thinking about how icky those lips stabbing her cheeks with their dry skin felt. Stephanie couldn't even scream.

The man caressed her breasts and told her he was real horny. "Do you know how to give head, baby? If you don't, you're about to learn."

She couldn't scream out because he had covered her mouth, so she silently prayed and asked God to help her. Suddenly, the guy whispered to her to get on her knees, as he zipped his pants down and forced her to the ground. Her knees hit the pavement with a thud. Her skin tore from her knees scraping the ground. He tried to guide her head to his private area. He pulled his sexual organ out, and it was pointed toward her face. She nearly passed out from the funk. Then he said, "Kiss it. You know you want to."

She balled her fist up with every ounce of strength she had and beat the crap out of the man's private member. She smacked hard at his private. The scum ball fell to the concrete ground with a thud. He was screaming and grabbing his exposed penis. People were pulling up in their cars and honking their horns.

To get the hysterical, swinging, crazy girl away from him, he kicked her in the head, knocking her out. Her head slammed against the ground, and the man got up and ran.

Witnesses were able to get a good description of the culprit. As passengers in their cars rushed to help the unconscious woman they had seen on many occasions in the building, someone called an ambulance and the police. Stephanie was knocked out cold and had blood running from her head.

She was rushed to the hospital and diagnosed with a concussion. The officer was there to take a report. Stephanie was so grateful she hadn't been raped or had other acts of sodomy forced on her. She continued to thank God.

She called Regina from the hospital. It didn't take her any time to get to her. As she told Regina what happened, she began to cry again. Regina just held her and let her express her pain through her tears.

Stephanie's phone rang. She looked down and saw it was Daniel. She gave the phone to Regina. "Talk to him."

"Hi, Pastor Winston." She told him what was going on.

"She doesn't want to talk. I'm going to take her home and then you can call her later. Wait one second, Pastor. That was the nurse. She said the doctor was going to keep Stephanie overnight for observation, since she has a head wound. "

Stephanie overheard him ask if it was okay to come to the hospital now. Regina looked at her and made a face. Stephanie smiled before continuing, "Sure, Pastor. You can come. We are at DePaul in Bridgeton."

The Pastor said a short prayer before leaving. "Please God, heal Stephanie and get me to the hospital in glory time."

****

Tabitha was lying across her bed. She spent most of her day crying and thinking about how Donnie threw her out of his office. He was so angry with her. Would she ever get him back? She wondered.

As she laid there, her phone rang. She saw the number. It was Jimmy. The job was successful. "I beat her butt good. Just like you said." He giggled. He sounded like he was intoxicated and kept laughing like he had something personal going on that was funny, but only he could hear it.

"You didn't hurt her too bad, did you?"

"I don't know, she was unconscious when I left. I want my money; I'm on my way to pick it up."

Jumping up from the bed, she shouted, "Don't come here. I'll meet you at the parking lot of McDonald's off Kings Highway at four p.m. Better yet, met me at 1400 Evans."

"I want two thousand dollars. If you don't want to be involved, I need a little more."

"I don't have that amount." She hit the table and the thumping sound vibrated against the wood.

"For what I went through, you're paying more, or else."

"Or else what? You did this. Not me."

"At your request. I recorded your request. I go down, so do you."

"I'm giving you four hundred and nothing more." Blowing out her breath, she added, "That's it. I don't have any more than that. I will see you at four."

After disconnecting the phone call, she walked through her trailer to the living area. Tabitha flopped down on the torn couch. "How could I be so stupid? I hope this crackhead don't get me sent up the river. Why on earth did I ever let myself get into something so silly that could be brought back to me?"

She turned on the television to view the news and to pass the time while she waited to meet Jimmy. As she flipped through the channels, she landed on Channel 4. They were covering the local news. The reporter was saying that the rapist had struck again. Tabitha turned the television up to listen, and once they repeated the location of the attempted rape, she knew it was Jimmy and Stephanie. This was bad. They were connecting the case with all the others, and she knew Jimmy wouldn't stand for that. He would demand more money and threaten her if she didn't give in.

She made a bad judgment call and had to do something about it. Her life was on the line, and without her freedom, she would lose Donnie forever. That wasn't a risk she was willing to take. If she were going to end up in jail, it would be for something far more horrible than hiring a hitman. Tabitha was doomed, and with that, so was Jimmy. Who would miss him anyway?

Chapter Nineteen

*P*astor Daniel Winston was in love. While he should have been celebrating, because he had finally met the one, he was scared, confused, and worried. He took this woman on and counseled her. She said a voice in her head sent her to the church for help. Was he helping her or helping himself? From the moment he met her, he wanted her. Was that normal? How many pastors had fallen in love with someone they were charged to help? What was he doing? Was he, in fact, helping himself to someone in distress?

It had been four months since she rushed through the doors of his church. Was that enough time to get over someone you promised to marry and love until death do them part? Was he blocking her from going back to a man she might still love? He was so conflicted. Maybe Elder Brown was right about him. But he had feelings for her. Pastor Winston couldn't get the beauty out of his mind or his heart. His dreams were filled with her smiling and kissing him. He was messed up and needed God.

He paced the floor back and forth. He had walked a path on his carpet in his study. Once he hung up the phone, after finding out Stephanie was in the hospital, he was worried. Why would someone want to hurt her? She seemed nice enough. She was helping the poor and needy. She had completed the Bible classes and was about to start coming to church and working on committees while waiting baptismal. So why would someone try to hurt her? Was it Donnie? After all, she refused to return to him.

Rearing back, he sat down on the big, wooden desk and stared at the white wall. His head was throbbing, trying to figure out why so much trouble was following this girl. He'd never heard of her until this all happened, and since the day he met her, all reports and surfing on the Internet suggested she was a good person and a bestselling author. She seemed popular in her community and had received many awards of recognition for her work and her books. So, what was going on with her and these adverse situations?

Pastor Daniel Winston was so lost. He stood up and moved from the desk. He postured himself for prayer. Bent down on his knees, he needed to talk to God. He was his source of hope, answers, and confirmation.

"Dear God," he breathed in, causing his chest to expand from the air. "I come to You with a heavy heart. I promised to serve You and not use the pulpit for bad. I have honored my words and commitment to You and the church. I have never sacrificed my soul for corruption, or used power against those who sought Your love and comfort. I have been faithful. But Lord, I have been lonely and praying for a helpmate. Until I met this young woman, I was content with occasionally dating because I knew, Lord, You would provide me with my need. I never doubt Your promise. I think I have found my soul and helpmate in this woman. You sent her here to this place for help, and the opportunity to renew her relationship with You. Please, Lord, guide me, so I won't go astray or allow my heart to get in the way of my service. If she is the one for me, I thank You, but if I am falling for the wrong one, guide me and heal my heart. Please Lord, bless her and heal anything that is hurting or bothering her. I thank You for saving her from harm today and every day. Thank You, Lord. Amen."

The love-struck preacher stood up and brushed his pant legs down. He strutted to his desk and made a phone call to his secretary and informed her of a couple of assignments he needed her to complete. "I'll be leaving for the day, Ms. Burton, but you know how to reach me if you need to."

Pastor Winston headed out the door to go visit Stephanie in the hospital. He'd asked God earlier to get him to the hospital in glory time. Apparently, God didn't want him to get there that fast because He slowed him down in order to think. He sensed a little peace, felt a bit stronger and had more hope that God would lead him. Pastor Winston got into his car and pulled off the parking lot, turning on the radio - one of his favorite songs was playing. Humming to himself, he tried to contain the Spirit of God enveloping him. Before he realized what was happening, tears were streaming down his face as he was singing, 'Though the storms keep on raging in my life. And sometimes it's hard to tell the night from day.' It was one of his favorite songs. It was the song, My Soul Has Been Anchored by Douglas Miller.

Pastor Winston couldn't understand what was happening to him and his heart. He was praying about it feverishly and asking God to forgive him for his thoughts because, Lord knows, this woman he was on his way to see had brought out feelings he had long buried when he lost his fiancé to a car accident almost five years ago. He thought back to that relationship and wondered if this was impacting him and his decisions.

He had met Pamela Martin more than seven years ago. They were both 28. They had met at a tent revival. It was a week-long service, and these pastors had come to town to teach everyone about the Sabbath. Pamela and her mom were there and so was Daniel. He knew about the Sabbath because that was the religion he grew up in, but he had long strayed away from when he left for college and found out about how wonderful life was living in the fast lane. Somewhere after graduating from college and becoming serious about his career, he began to think about his future, and that included bringing God back into his life.

It was on Wednesday when he met her. It was his fourth day at the revival and her first. She sat next to him, and that started up a conversation, which led him to ask her for a date two nights later.

Theirs was a beautiful courtship with so many plans. He fell hard for the nurse, and she loved him dearly. They joined church and were baptized together. He loved her so much that he would call her often to check on her. Never had his heart been so warm, so loved, and so thankful. They planned their wedding for the following year, and their parents were excited. Unfortunately, they would never marry. Pamela fell asleep and lost control of her car, after working a double shift, and never regained consciousness.

For a while, Daniel was angry. He left the church for a year. But God doesn't play that. He had plans for the young man. He was supposed to fall in love and experience that kind of hurt and pain. Daniel was in so much pain after he lost Pamela, he sought counseling and group therapy. After some time spent healing, he volunteered to help others who had been through the exact thing: losing a loved one. This became his specialty. After having a successful technology business, he sold his company and went to divinity school. He received a Master's in theology and counseling, eventually getting his license to practice. This is where he honed his pastoral and counseling skills. Now, he was sought out by others to help hurting and brokenhearted loved ones. God knew what His plans were for Daniel and when he came to understand that, he grew in his spiritual life. But even after all that, he still had never found the kind of love he shared with Pamela. He'd gone on dates, but the thought of marriage and children didn't enter his mind until he saw Stephanie and suffered that jolt of electricity that bolted from her fingertips to his hands. That spark jolted his heart in a way that he couldn't understand nor control, and here he was on his way to see the woman that hit his heart with a powerful surge of love and desire. Only God could stop him from loving her now.

"I need You, Lord. But mostly, Lord, I ask that You protect my heart from pain. If she is not the one You have prepared for me, help me to understand and not allow me to fall back into the depression I suffered from the loss of Pamela. I don't think I could handle that."

Chapter Twenty

*J*immy danced with joy. He allowed his tongue to run across his dry lips and jiggled his legs to the beat of his heart. Jimmy only became this excited when money entered the picture, and he would become the beneficiary. He bounced to the imaginary beat in his head, due to the simple fact that he had hit a payday without doing any real work. This would give him enough money to catch up on his bills and to celebrate with a hit or two of crack. Who would've thought it would be so easy to make a couple grand in less than 30 minutes? One thing for sure, no jealous and insecure women would lay their dirty fingers on his dough. Those dirt daubers would do anything to keep a man and take their money. Even if that man didn't want to be kept by the woman. Other women would do anything to keep a man, like kill or destroy their property. Jimmy loved drugs, so to secure them, he did whatever it took to find the money to pay for them.

In the past two months, Jimmy made over five thousand dollars, jumping on women for other women who were looking for revenge. He didn't like hurting women, but heck, he needed a job and money... and right now. No one offered him anything - a job, a handout, nothing. People called him a crackhead, but in his mind, he represented businessmen. With no job, he had no money, and without the funds, he had no drugs. He refused to go down like that. His plan would milk Tabitha out of all the money he could.

He didn't start out this way. He once owned a car wash. He made a lot of money and met a lot of women, but they were his downfall.

The women stole his money and introduced him to crack. Once that happened, his life, company, and everything he touched went downhill. For that reason, he hurt women because they hurt him. They destroyed him. Once he finished with Tabitha, he would destroy her too. Anger and regret filled his heart and getting even with others brought new life into his dying soul. Revenge served cold cured his pain.

When people hurt, they hurt others. That adage bored Jimmy, and he tired easily from hearing folks reference it, so he laughed about it. It didn't mean crap to him until he experienced it. When you meet the wrong one, with venom and hate in their soul - if you're not careful and leave - that very one will destroy you. That's what happened to Jimmy. He gave her everything, and she took and took until nothing lingered. Eventually, she encouraged him to try crack, and he did, for her. But that one mistake he would always regret. Jimmy witnessed the power of the drug and saw the damage it did to so many other folks. But he, like everyone who did drugs and lost, believed the same thing. He believed he could win the war on using. A confident man, he assumed his innate ability gave him the strength needed to resist temptation because his disposition made him different and stronger than others. No drug or no woman would cause him to fail. He exceeded the words and abilities of simple men. But drugs had no boundaries between any person, clean or otherwise. If you are tough enough, give it a try, and once drugs show you how good it can make you feel, you become a runner who does nothing but run to find more. Using drugs introduced folks to the devil himself; and for Jimmy, the power of meeting him tempted him over and over. He acted like the devil himself when high. But once those devilish drugs sought you out, captured your soul and heart, you were hooked. Once he hooks you, God is the only person who can save you.

Jimmy didn't go to church and didn't believe in God. Although, word on the street was that God can help you when all else fails. Drugs increased his strength, not this God, and he would do whatever it took just to feel the lift it gave.

When he hit crack, it fondled his mind like psychedelic colors, rainbows, and raindrops on a hot, soaking, sweaty day, cooling off your burned skin. You underwent pure joy, like you were stronger, better and prettier than God. He sat on the creaky, old steps of an abandoned house waiting for someone to come by with some crack. His hands shook, and he stared at the ground. Suddenly, he jumped off the steps and started to run. Running became his new reward for weight loss. Jimmy ran just about every day. He dashed off the porch to run from an enraged drug dealer, whom he still owed money to from the last time he begged for credit.

Broke from purchasing drugs to save his life, he dashed like an Olympic medal winner in a 400-meter race. Age and drugs slowed him down, and he couldn't run as fast as he used to back before substance use took over. Skinny and frail, Jimmy squeezed through a fence and got away. "Man, I told you I would give your money to you." He pivoted around and screamed, as he scaled another fence. Suddenly, the air around him caressed his face when something zoomed by his ear. That dude tried to shoot me, he thought. He only owed him 90 dollars. To be murdered over chump change angered and amazed him. Why lose your life for something so petty? After all, if he died, didn't they both lose? Jimmy loss to the graveyard and the shooter to prison. No one gained anything but a loss of living.

"Let me catch you, boy. You all mine." The dealer screamed and then shot off several more bullets.

Huffing and puffing, Jimmy ran between houses and then he stopped to catch his breath. "Old dude is trying to kill me. Man, life must be better than this. I gotta change, or I will die as a crackhead."

Once he sensed the threat had been eliminated, Jimmy rummaged into his pockets and found his government-issued phone. "Tabitha." He screamed into the phone. "I want two thousand dollars." He decided to die for ninety dollars alluded to much more than being stupid. Due to that alone, he needed an increase for the dirty deed she asked him to do.

"I told you, Jimmy, I'm only giving you four hundred dollars and you better not ask for one dime more."

"You talking like you running things."

"I am. I don't think you want me to tell Doug, the dealer, where to find you; now do you?"

"Okay. I'll take the money. When can I pick it up?" He stood up after bending down to catch his breath.

"Sounds like you been running." Tabitha laughed.

"Where's my money?" His voice boomed through the phone.

"Meet me on the corner of 1400 Evans. I'm going to pull up in a Jeep. You walk up, and I will toss the money to you. Be there at 7:00 tonight." She ended the call.

Chapter Twenty-One

*P*astor Winston arrived at the hospital and proceeded to walk in. Two women stopped him at the door. They were his parishioners. "Good morning, ladies."

"Hi, Pastor," the ladies sang in unison, as they batted their fake eyelashes. "What are you doing here?" Sandra Jensen asked.

"Visiting the sick," he responded, as they prepared to walk away.

"Who is sick? Is it one of our members?"

"You can come visit me anytime, Pastor," Jamie Johnson said, as she slithered over and wrapped her arms around his. "When are we going to go out? I'm interested in you."

"Sis Johnson, the Bible says, 'Whoso findeth a wife findeth a good thing, and obtaineth favour of the LORD.'"

"That don't mean nothing to me, Pastor." She squeezed his arm tighter.

Pulling away, he said, "It means something to me though. Let the man ask for a date and let him do his bidding. That way, you will understand he's interested in you. I pray you experience a blessed day, but I must run to check on the person I came to visit. Be blessed sisters." The pastor turned and walked away, leaving both ladies standing and wondering what happened.

"Girl, ain't nobody thinking about what he just said. That handsome brother better keep eyes on his forehead and his back. I want him, and you can bet Jamie gets what she wants." She pulled her skirt down and pivoted, walking out of the hospital.

Sandra responded, "I don't blame you for wanting him. He's fair game, since he's not married."

****

Pastor asked for the room number for Stephanie Whitmore from the attendant at the front desk greeting visitors. She gave him room number 458, and he proceeded to the elevators. Before getting on the elevator, he spotted a gift shop and went in to purchase some fresh flowers. After paying the clerk, he journeyed back to the elevator up to the fourth floor. Once on the fourth floor, he walked into the room and found Stephanie sleeping. He put the flowers on the table beside her bed and stood over her, silently praying for her health. As he prayed, he took her hand into his, and she squeezed his hand. Once he finished the prayer, he looked at her and smiled. "Hi, beautiful."

"Hi," Stephanie said. Her smile shined bright like a lit chandelier, and her face seemed to glow, even with the wrap that surrounded her forehead and part of her head.

"Are you in any pain?" He wanted to find out as he gazed at her.

"Not really. The nurses gave me some pain medicine, so I'm fine. They'll let me leave tomorrow. They wanted to run some tests to make sure no other issues existed. My head hit the ground pretty hard."

"Did they find who did this to you?" He bent over closer to her.

"Not to my knowledge. That was so scary. But I prayed and asked God to save me, and He did."

"God is in the blessing business, and I'm so glad He is. I'm so thankful He answered your prayers. Otherwise, I would be a devastated man."

"Really, Daniel?" Stephanie couldn't contain the smile spreading across her face.

"Yes. Really. We are just getting comfortable with each other, and the devil tries this. He won't win, Stephanie, but stay in prayer because he'll keep trying. Whenever someone is turning their lives over to God, the devil gets straight to business trying to detour them. But prayer is everything, and God will help us fight our battles, and that includes with Satan." He squeezed her hand and then brought them up to his face and kissed the back of her hand.

"I'm grateful. I thank God for being there with me. That man reeked of drugs and even though he acted alone in that garage, the presence of God resided in me. Thank you so much for reminding me about the Bible during Bible study. I learned about it as a child, but I hadn't studied in years."

"Thankfully, you listened to God, Stephanie, when you came to our church. As a matter-of-fact, I'm so glad you did."

"Me too," Stephanie said, as she lifted her body up into an upright position. "What are you doing today?"

"I must make a home visit to one of the Deaconess of the church. She is ill and resting at home. I'm going to pray for her."

"Do you become tired, Daniel I mean, you do a lot of work inside the church and outside. Then you visit folks, and you teach classes. How do you do it all?"

"Sometimes, I do. But my elders and assistant pastor help me when I can't spread myself so far. I also pray, rest, and let God lead me. I cannot do all things, but through God, I can do many things."

"That's good, Pastor. I'm glad you came by. But this medicine is making me sleepy." She released his hand and pulled the covers up. He helped her to cover her body, bent down, and gently kissed her lips. "I'm leaving, but I will call you later, if you don't mind."

"I don't mind. I'll talk to you later. Stephanie closed her eyes and slept peacefully. Pastor Winston prayed loudly for Stephanie and asked God to continue to pour blessings on her. When he finished, he kissed her cheek and left.

Chapter Twenty-Two

*D*onnie sat at his desk and reminisced about Stephanie. He experienced so much anger due to his life. He wondered about that dude at Stephanie's house. *Did she like him? Was it too late for him to win her back? It had only been four months. Was she seeing him before they broke up?*

"How dare she act all innocent in this mess," He spoke out loudly. "Women are so messy, and yet they try to act so innocent. If she never dated that dude, where did he get the courage to stand in her home and act like the protector?"

He stood up and walked to the window. That day started out so exciting, and together, he and Kent had such a good time. Kent hoped Stephanie would want to spend time with the two of them, but she refused. Being mean to a kid never would have been a character trait of the girl he loved. She allowed a man to come between her love for Kent and him. He strutted back to his desk and picked up the phone. He had to keep trying. He needed her. He dialed her number, but it just rang.

He decided to complete some paperwork, and then he tried her number again. Still, it just rang. Then his phone rang. Without looking, he grabbed it, "Hey, Stephanie."

"Is that all you think about... her?" Tabitha popped her gum into the phone.

Donnie hated that about her. She was always smacking and popping gum, and to him, that was so ghetto. He'd messed up bad messing around with Tabitha, and now it seemed he couldn't make her disappear. How would he rid himself of her presence?

"What do you want?"

"What we had, Donnie. I miss you."

"Tabitha, we didn't mean anything to each other." He drummed his fingers on the desk and blew the air out of his mouth that he had been holding in, listening to her talk about nothing.

"Yes we did, Donnie. When we were making love, you said you loved me. Now, you're acting crazy."

"I'm acting crazy, Tabitha? I don't think so. I told you to leave me alone, but you keep calling and showing up at my job. There is nothing going on. We were friends with benefits."

"Is that right? You really think you can shake me a loose by telling me that now? Well, not this time, Donnie. You left me with a little present, and we are forever bonded."

"Don't play with me, Tabitha. I mean it. Don't freaking play with me." He was angry. He slammed his fist on the desk.

A loud bang rang in Tabitha's ear. It was the sound of a fist hitting the desk. "Dang, my hand," he called out. She could tell he walloped the desk hard by the way he screamed. The sound vibrated against her ear. But she had to do what she had to do. "I'm pregnant, Donnie. You're going to be a father."

"Do away with it. I don't want anything to do with you or that baby." He hated to say what he was saying. He didn't believe or support abortions. He didn't want to kill a child, especially his, but he couldn't trust this backwoods woman. He understood now why a man should never stick his private into someone they couldn't live with, but it was too late for him. He hoped she lied about being pregnant by him.

"Lord, help me," he murmured.

"I'm not having an abortion. Either you marry me or plan to pay big bucks for child support. What you make, about two hundred thousand a year? Well, that's about two thousand dollars a month for me. Now, you can either pay me or marry me. Remember, I'm cheaper to keep." She was hoping her lie was working. She could marry him and become pregnant later.

"Listen here. I'm not marrying a hillbilly, and you can believe that. Don't call this number again unless you're asking for money to do away with that baby. Keep in mind, I'm not paying you jack. I don't believe you're pregnant by me, and if you are, I'm willing to do a DNA test. But as I informed, I will not participate in anything to do with you or a baby." He hung up the phone.

"Lord, forgive me. I cannot let her force a baby on me. What kind of life would my child live? Please, Lord. Don't let her be pregnant by me. Stephanie would never forgive me."

Donnie laid his head on his desk and waited on Stephanie to call him. At some point, he fell asleep, and when he awakened, he realized that it was dark out. Apparently, his secretary had left thinking he was gone for the day. He stood up and stretched his legs. He reached up high and did the same to his body. "That stretch was excellent." But still, he had a problem. He prayed Tabitha was lying. He didn't gather much information about her, except that she said her mother was an alcoholic and she'd had a terrible childhood. She always talked about getting away from their trailer, but to him she was repeating her mom's situation by moving into her own trailer home. He begged God for mercy and to stop her from birthing a child by him. She had never even attended college.

He picked up the phone and pushed his favorite button.

Stephanie picked up, "Donnie, please stop. Please. I'm not coming back. I don't love you."

"That cannot be true. You accepted my hand and agreed to marry me. You wouldn't do that if you didn't love me. Why are you saying that? I messed up. But I've learned my lesson." He sat down on the arm of his large, burgundy, leather chair.

"Listen. I don't love you. That ended when I caught you. Please, leave me alone. I don't want to involve the law again, Donnie. Our relationship is over."

When he spoke again, it was to dead air. She had ended the call. His life was over. They always said you never missed people until they were gone. His heart was broken, and it was no one's fault but his. Now, he had to figure out how to win her back or live without her. Life without Stephanie couldn't be an option.

Chapter Twenty-Three

*T*abitha prepared to take the money to Jimmy. She went to her closet and pulled out her gun. She didn't trust that drug addict. He was dangerous, and she refused to visit him without her protection. She was thinking of killing him because she knew he would always blackmail her about her role in what he did to Stephanie. Before she would go to jail, she would take him out. After all, no one would miss him. Plus, he was a wanted man. He owed so many drug dealers money and they were all looking for him. She laughed, as she thought about how fast that skinny man could run.

Tabitha put the gun in her purse and grabbed her keys. She hoped it wouldn't be necessary to kill anyone, but for her freedom, she would do what she had to do. She strutted out the front door and got into her Jeep. "Soon, I'll buy a new one when Donnie starts paying me child support." She laughed so loud the sound stunned her eardrums. The voice that echoed in the air sounded like a hyena in despair.

She glanced at her gold timepiece that Donnie had given her and observed it was almost 6:30 p.m. She had 30 minutes to arrive at Evans Street to meet with Jimmy. She reached for the door and pulled it open.

This transaction had to run smoothly. She didn't want any problems, or anyone to notice her with this druggie. She tossed her purse over to the passenger's seat. Starting her Jeep, Tabitha backed out into the street and gunned the motor. She wanted this over and was sorry she even stooped so low to become involved with Jimmy. Her only wish was that this creep had sense enough to prevent himself from getting caught and ratting her out.

As she drove, she hummed and rocked her head to the oldie but goodie, "I'm Stone in Love with You" by The Stylistics.

"Sing that song," she screamed, raising her voice. She loved the Stylistics, and today's singers wished they had the talents of the older generation of excellent musicians. She enjoyed the cool, melodic singing of the old groups that needed no fine auto-tuning. She stopped at the signal as the light eased from yellow to red.

Tabitha reached over and patted her gun. She couldn't chance going to meet Jimmy without it. Knowing she had money on her was like winning the lottery for a junkie who didn't mind hurting someone for one more hit.

Tabitha saw the sign for Evans and made a right turn. She chose this neighborhood because it was ghetto and drugs were sold out in the open to customers. She believed that if anything happened here, the police wouldn't look too hard to find out what happened, because losing a druggie to violence was like saving the tax payers dollars by not having court and throwing someone behind bars.

She drove down the street until she found an area with no people around, pulled up, and waited. It was 6:50 p.m. She eased the motor off and then decided to turn it back on. She couldn't risk the old, beat up Jeep not starting if she had to leave the scene to flee from danger.

She reared back, relaxed and counted to 10. Then, she reached over, pulled out the envelope with the money in it, and grabbed her gun. Taking the safety lock off, she positioned the gun in her right hand, so she would be prepared should anything happen. At 7:00 p.m., she looked at her wristwatch and turned to her right at the light tap on her closed car window.

"What's up, Tabitha? Where's my money?"

Tabitha looked up and giggled at the frail-looking, once handsome Jimmy. His nose was running, and he had a black eye with dried blood on the side of his face. She rolled her window down and asked, "Who you pissed off to the point they beat your butt?"

"Just give me my money so I can leave as fast as I came. You best be glad I'm not asking for more."

"When I give this to you, I don't want to entertain your pitiful self again." She raised her gun to make sure he understood she meant business.

"You don't scare me—"

But before Jimmy could utter another word, his blood splattered all over her, as he fell into her window. In a panic, she screamed, pushed him off her car and pulled off. Her heart pounded so hard it was as if it had exploded in her chest. Fear swaddled her like a blanket. As she sped away and looked into her rearview mirror, she spotted two men walk up to Jimmy and shoot him again.

She prayed the guys didn't recognize her or remember the license plate number on her old Jeep. Though she was terrified, the further she drove from the scene, the calmer she became and a little glee bubbled in her soul, knowing that he could not report that she hired him to beat up Stephanie.

Thankfully, she still had her money. It was going to be a significant sacrifice to hand that money over, but now Jimmy was gone and she had enough money to pay a couple more months of rent. Life was good. Her problem had disappeared, and soon she would be getting Donnie back. One thing she knew about him was that he loved children. Being pregnant would draw him right into the web she was weaving for him, and if anyone got in her way... just like Jimmy... they would be dead as he was laying in the street in his blood. Nothing would come between her and Donnie, and she meant that.

Chapter Twenty-Four

*P*astor Winston dressed and left for the hospital to pick up Stephanie. They had spoken on the phone the previous night, and she said the doctor would be releasing her by 12:30 p.m. She had a concussion, but she was fine. The doctor recommended she receive counseling to deal with the trauma she had experienced.

Pastor arrived at 12:00 noon, as agreed on by them both. He strolled through the hospital with a new lease on life. His steps had a bigger purpose, his walk jollier; he was a happy man.

The pastor moved toward her room, and the floor nurse recognized him and spoke. "Hey, Pastor Winston. How are you?"

"Hello, Ms. Jamison, right?" He reached out his hand to greet her. "We meet again."

"Yes, we do, and this is a welcomed surprise. Are you here to visit a member of your church?" She was hoping he was there to ask her out. She was very attracted to the pastor and had observed him on many occasions at the hospital visiting his sick and shut-in.

"I'm here to pick up a friend. But be blessed." He turned and walked to Stephanie's room. He could still feel Ms. Jamison's eyes on him and wondered how long it would be before he could announce to the world he was in love.

Pastor Winston walked into Stephanie's room and found her sitting in a wheelchair. A smile crept across his face. Stephanie did that to him. Whenever she was in his presence, he couldn't stop smiling.

He felt good around her. His insides bubbled with joy.

He strutted over to her and bent down and kissed her gently on the lips. "Hi, Beautiful. You ready to roll?"

Stephanie's eyes beamed, and at the same time, her eyeballs seemed to sparkle. "Hi, Daniel. Yes, I am ready to roll. Let me call the nurse to inform her that you're here." She reached for the remote to summon the nurse. As soon as she pressed the button with the picture of the nurse on it, Nurse Jamison walked in.

"Hi, Ms. Whitmore. You are all prepped and ready to go?" Nurse Jamison eye balled the pastor. Although she was talking to the patient, her eyes were speaking to the handsome man standing in front of her. "The transporter will be here in about five minutes to take you down."

"Pastor Winston can take me." Stephanie turned to face the nurse, who was so busy staring at the pastor, she didn't hear the patient. "Uhh, excuse me, if you can break away from the pastor, I was saying, he can roll me to the car."

A little embarrassed that she was caught, but happy the pastor knew she was into him, Nurse Jamison responded, "No, I'm sorry, the transporter has to do it. Hospital rules." She turned back to the pastor. "I do hope you'll grace our floor again." Turning back to Stephanie, she said, "You take care of yourself, and please do be careful. People are so evil and uncaring today."

Stephanie smiled. "Thank you, Nurse, for your care." Stephanie was intrigued that so many women were after the pastor. She was impressed by how calm he was when women responded to him so openly.

Nurse Jamison started to walk out. "Bye, Pastor," she waved, as she sashayed out the door.

"Wow, Daniel. How do you do it and stay on the straight and narrow with God? I mean, all these women pushing themselves on you, and they are beautiful."

"Stephanie, our strength comes from God, and through Him, I can do all things. I'm following His lead and allowing Him to direct my path. And Stephanie, I love where He is leading me to."

A smile crept on her face, and she said, "Me too." Then she allowed the transporter, who had entered the room, to push her to her destination.

The pastor went to retrieve his car while the transporter stayed and waited with Stephanie. Once the pastor returned, and Stephanie was in the car, he drove her home.

When they arrived at her house, he helped her onto the couch. Stephanie asked, "Are you staying with me?" She pushed herself back into the pillows to become more comfortable.

Contemplating what to say, he took a deep breath and said, "No. I scheduled several appointments."

Crossing her legs and looking up into his eyes, she asked, "Are you coming back?"

"I'm not sure. Do you need anything?" He walked over and sat next to her. Turning to face her, he took her face into his hands and looked into her eyes. "Are you okay with being here?"

"No. My parents are out of town again, and my friend left this morning going back to Los Angeles on a business trip. I didn't want to alarm her. She had to go to court to handle a case. My parents are returning in a couple of days. I told them I was ok. Although physically, I am, I don't think I am mentally. I'm a little afraid to be here alone." Feeling a little embarrassed, she rubbed her bare shoulder. "I'm sorry to worry you."

"You're not worrying me, but I have an idea. Let me call Deaconess Perkins and see if she can stay with you for a few days, or maybe you can spend a couple of nights with her. I believe you met her, right?" He paused and waited for her reply.

"Yes. She was one of the Bible workers who came by weekly."

He proceeded to dial her number. "Is it okay with you?"

"I guess so. She may not want to stay."

"Let me check. She's a nurse, and she has stayed with many church members while they healed." He finished dialing her number.

After he was connected with her on the phone, he explained the situation to her, and she agreed to come and stay with Stephanie. "This is great. She will be here in a couple of hours. She said don't cook; she will do that when she gets here."

"Daniel are you sure she doesn't mind?" She looked up at him.

"If I didn't think she would do it, I wouldn't have called her. She's a solid Christian, and this is her mission. She would never agree if she didn't want to do it. Besides, she's said some awesome things about you."

"Oh, really?" Stephanie perked up a bit. Her shoulders lifted high and the smile that had dashed off her face made a quick run to land back in place.

"Yes, she thinks you are quite extraordinary, very smart and a wise girl; and she said you were quite beautiful and charming." He sat down and took her left hand and kissed the back of it. "Stephanie, you are going to be just fine. I think you'll enjoy her company."

"I trust you. Thank you for picking me up and arranging for someone to stay with me. I really do appreciate it." She leaned over and kissed his lips, quickly, but he leaned in and gave her a deeper kiss. When he released her, she was so deep into her feelings for him she just stared until he kissed her on the cheek and left.

Chapter Twenty-Five

*D*onnie dialed Stephanie's number and was surprised she finally answered. "What you been up to lately? I have been trying to reach you for two days." He released a mouthful of air. It seemed like time stopped and he had been holding it in for hours.

"I was in the hospital." Before she could utter another word, he panicked.

"Are you okay? What happened? Talk to me, baby." His words flowed out of his mouth so fast, it was like slushing. It made you think of water rushing to the beach and splashing on the people.

"Slow down, man. First, I'm not your baby. But to make a long story short, I was attacked in my parking lot at work."

"Oh, my God. You were the person they were talking about on the news a couple of days ago?"

"Yes. But I'm okay." She reared her back into the plush pillows behind her.

"I wish I'd catch the person who did this to you. I promise he won't get an opportunity to hurt anyone else." He relaxed and sat down at his kitchen table. He tossed a grape into his mouth. "May I come by to see you?"

"Donnie, no. Nothing has changed with us. Let it go, please. You are wearing me down."

"That's what I want to do, baby." He ate another grape.

"But you won't be successful at wearing me down. That situation will not happen like that for you. I'm seeing someone else, and I like him."

Standing up and walking around he stated, "Rebound lust like that don't last. You are wasting time with that brother. You don't fall out of love that quick."

"Okay, Donnie. I'm not going to argue with you, but you and I haven't been together in nearly five months. Plus, what you did, cannot be forgotten. I have forgiven you, but the relationship is over. You take care of yourself."

Before Donnie could utter another word, he heard nothing. No air, no sound, nothing. That's just how he felt too, like nothing. It hurt his heart to accept that he had lost the love of his life.

Just as he tried to gather his senses, his doorbell rang. He put his cellphone down and sauntered to the massive, wooden door. He grabbed the golden door knob and pulled it open.

"What do you want?" He asked with urgency and ignorance when he saw Tabitha standing there. She walked in and he slammed the door.

"Don't shatter your windows. Being angry is not going to help our situation." Tabitha went into the living room and sat down on the brown leather couch.

"We need to discuss our baby."

Slamming his hand on the counter, Donnie yelled, "There is no baby, stop lying." He rushed into the living room and screamed, "Don't play with me."

She flinched. "I have never seen you like this. I pray you don't do anything to me. I don't need you behind bars, the baby has needs. If you are behind the wall, we will both suffer."

"Lord, how did I find myself in this messed up situation?"

"Well, just understand you're too late to call on God. You should have done that before we slept together. You knew that by sleeping with me unprotected this could happen."

"I thought you would handle that."

"Yeah, right. I did, but the birth control did not work. You men need to protect yourselves from having babies when you claim you don't want them." She stood up. "I need some money. I have to eat healthier and buy my prenatal vitamins."

He reached into his pocket. "Here, take this and purchase an abortion. You are not my wife, and I'm not about to have a baby by someone like you." He threw five one hundred-dollar bills at her.

"What do you mean someone like me? You slept with me. I guess I was good enough for sex, but not to be your wife or to have your child?"

"You said it." He turned his back and walked away. Tabitha rushed and jumped on his back and started beating him in the head with her fists. "Take that back. Take that back."

He tried to remove her from his back gently, but she was thrashing and flailing her arms all over his body. He backed up to the couch and dumped her.

Tabitha was breathing hard and screaming.

He looked down at her with disgust. "Stop all that noise, or I'm calling the police."

Tabitha stopped crying and screaming long enough to bend down and pick up the money. "I'll be back, and this is not sufficient. You will have to pay me child support, and I'm pretty sure it will be closer to three thousand a month. So, you need to set up something to automatically pay me. Get ready. You played, and now you are going to have to pay. Now, if you want to marry me, we can talk." She grabbed her purse and headed out the door. Before she closed the door behind her, she turned and showed him the gun she had. "Thankfully, I didn't have to use this on my child's father. Tread lightly with me, darling. I'm hormonal and hurt. That's a dangerous combination." She slammed the door.

Chapter Twenty-Six

*T*abitha was sitting in her car listening to the local radio station. The disc jockey was talking about all the killings that were happening in St. Louis and was pleading for the gangs to stop slaughtering people, especially, innocent bystanders.

"Please stop the killing. This is getting out of hand. To shoot a man in broad daylight, in the middle of the street, with witnesses everywhere is crazy. Please stop this." The jock was pleading, and you could hear the distress in his voice. "Drugs have taken over our communities, and those who are pushing the poison are also killing people. The person who shot Jimmy Taylor ought to be ashamed of themselves. He couldn't hurt you because he was too sick and strung out on drugs. He was a successful businessman who used to help the community. But no, y'all don't remember that."

Tabitha chuckled and said out loud, "That brother was a crackhead. No need to cry for him. If they did not kill him, I would have probably done it myself. You cannot play with fire and expect not to get burned. People need to stop. Folks are tired of playing with these folks."

She pulled up in front of a liquor store to buy herself some gin and a pack of cigarettes. When she walked out, she saw a woman who looked just like Donnie's ex-fiancée. She took another look and laughed, "Nah, that ain't her. She looks better than that dumb heifer." She laughed and decided she needed to get rid of Stephanie. Donnie would love her if she was out of the way.

Ever since Stephanie dumped him for being unfaithful, he had changed. He'd become mean, angry at the world, and blamed her for their breakup. That was the one thing she didn't understand about men. They messed around, played the field, dipped into other women's goody-pot and when they got caught, instead of accepting the blame, they acted like someone did them wrong. But Tabitha wasn't having it. She was going to make sure something happened to Stephanie because she loved Donnie. But more than anything, she loved what he could do for her financially. Being with him could put her into a higher class. Nothing would stop her from benefitting and having a better life, especially not that skinny, annoying, monkey-looking woman who had her man's heart. She was going to set some things into motion that would drop Donnie to his knees and make him come running back to her.

Tabitha got into her car, put the key into the ignition, and started it. She tried to turn on her air, but nothing happened. "Dang. I'm sick of this raggedy car." She banged on the steering wheel. Rolling her window down, she lit her cigarette and opened her bottle of gin and took several swallows. "Ahhh... that hit the spot." She beat her chest gently to help the liquor go down smoothly. Taking another sip, she admitted, "That's so good."

She grabbed her cell and put the cigarette in the ashtray. She went into her contacts and found her enemy's name and pressed send. The phone rang and Stephanie picked up.

"Hey, this is Donnie's fiancée, Tabitha. I'm calling to let you know that I'm pregnant by him and I want you to leave us alone."

"You're what?" Stephanie sat up on the couch, trying to make sure she heard her right. She should have blocked her number but decided to wait. It was better to know a person's plan who was at odds with you then not to know.

"Pregnant by Donnie's and I'm his fiancée. Act like you know me, skank."

Tabitha could feel the liquor taking effect. She was feeling bolder, calmer, and like she could fight a bull. "Woman, you know who this is. It's Tabitha. Now, don't get your little, skinny butt hurt. I don't play. I'm warning you."

"You don't have any issues with me. I'm not your problem. He is. I don't want your man; he wants me. Please tell him to stop calling me, and since you are pregnant and he loves children, I'm sure you can have him all to your little self. So please, don't call here anymore." She hung up the phone. She whispered, "Lord, help me. I'm so tired of this mess. Help a sister out, Lord."

Sister Jenkins heard her praying and walked over to the couch. "Are you okay?"

Releasing the air from her lungs, in frustration, she answered, "I'm trying. But that negative situation that brought me to your church keeps coming back full force, trying to stop me from my pursuit of happiness with God."

Taking her hand and patting it, Sister Jenkins assured her, "Well, we are not going to let anything interrupt your relationship with God. Let's pray about it." And they did.

Once the prayer was over, Stephanie felt calm and as if God had stepped into the situation and was cleaning up her problems. She reached over and kissed Sister Jenkins on her cheek. "Thank you so much for staying with me and for your prayers. I appreciate you more than you know."

****

Tabitha looked at the phone and saw that Stephanie had ended the call. "No, that heifer didn't hang up on me." Now she was outraged and felt that she was being disrespected. She laid her head into the torn, leather headrest and closed her eyes.

"Dirty, Dirty, Dirty, Dirty Tab-by. Funky, Funky, Dirty Tab-by." The kids were circling her singing loud and laughing at her. "Stinky, Stinky, Stinky Tabitha." She started hitting her head against the headrest. Banging harder, she spoke, "Nah, I will not be dismissed like that. I will not be rejected by Ms. Goodie Two-Shoes. Her butt is mine. She has messed with the wrong one, and I'm going to make her pay."

Tabitha screamed and pulled into traffic, barely missing an oncoming car. She lifted her hand up and gave the driver the finger. She hollered out to the woman, "You whore."

Chapter Twenty-Seven

Sister Clay picked up the phone and called the office of the Metropolitan Ministerial Alliance for Ministers. She wanted to hear what the results of their decision was after she met with them. Would she be able to go back to her church home? Even though she said she didn't want to go back, she did. She asked for Pastor Jayson, who headed the Ministerial Alliance.

When Pastor Jayson picked up the phone, Sister Clay reminded him who she was.

"Hi, Pastor, I wanted to know your decision about me returning to True Church. This is Sister Clay, and I must've missed your call to me, since there are no messages from you all. As a matter-of-fact, I shouldn't have to call you all for a report, you should be calling me. Especially, since you all claim to help people." She cleared her throat.

"Sister Clay, we were scheduled to call you. We decided..."

Before he could get the words out of his mouth, Sister Clay started screaming, "I knew it. I knew you would side with him. You all are on the same team." She smacked her lips.

"Sister, I didn't get out what I was about to say. We don't think you should attend a church where you are not happy and don't trust the leaders. There are too many churches out here, and we are confident you can find another place to worship that will bring you peace."

"Yeah, I knew you all would pull this game. I wasted my time coming to talk to you all. You're all on the same team - Satan's."

Frustrated, she hung up the phone. She stood up and paced back and forth on the linoleum floor. Stopping in her tracks, she slammed her fist into the white, kitchen wall. "Oh, my God, that hurts." She shook her hand out trying to shake off the pain. With tears leaking from her eyes, she vowed, "I will not be defeated."

Pastor Jayson held the phone and looked to see if Sister Clay had ended the call. "My goodness, that whippersnapper hung up on me. She didn't give me an opportunity to even talk." He sat back down at the table where he was meeting with several other ministers. "You all wouldn't believe this. I tried to explain to Sister Clay about our decision, and she straight went off on me. That's sad too, because I could have prayed for her and provided her with the proper guidance."

"Well, Pastor," the pastor from Jericho Baptist said, "We cannot save everybody, only God can. We've done our spiritual duty. Ms. Clay will have to bear her cross and pray and ask God to lead her. I just pray she realizes she is the problem."

Pastor Brunson of St. Peter's Temple said, "You're right about that. She must find her way; and with prayer, she will."

The pastors prayed for Sister Clay and other parishioners, and then they went on to the next order of business.

****

Sister Clay picked up the phone and called her friend. "Hey, Sister Green."

"Hey, Girl. How are you this fine morning?" Sister Green was happy to hear from her old friend. They hadn't spoken in a month.

"Girl, I'm fine. Oh, wait a minute. I was great until I talked to that false prophet Pastor Jayson." Sister Clay smacked her lips and hissed. "Do you know what they did?"

Sitting down and preparing for this conversation, Sister Green rubbed her temple. This friendship took so much work, but she loved her friend. She had known Sister Clay for more than 20 years, and she wasn't always so negative and mean. A bad marriage had sent her world tumbling down about 10 years ago, and ever since that happened, she was on a mission to make everyone else pay for her unhappiness.

"No, I don't." She said it slow, with some hesitancy. "What did they say?"

"Absolutely nothing. Just that I would be happier somewhere else is what he insinuated. I got so mad, I just hung up on Pastor Fake Jayson." She sat down at her kitchen table, grabbed her coffee, and took a sip. "I tell you. God is going to make these false prophets pay for misleading and harming His flock."

"Well, sis, think about it this way. Maybe all this was for the best. Why worship where you are not welcomed? The church is a place you should be able to find some peace, but since you burned your bridges there—"

Jumping up out of her seat, Sister Clay said, "What do you mean I burned my bridges there? Are you crazy or sipping on liquor?"

"Now, you know I don't drink." Sister Green rubbed her forehead, trying to release the tension that was building.

"You're acting like it, making a statement like that. I have the right to worship wherever I want to, and no man will stop me." Sister Clay sat back down and tapped her fingers on the cherry wood, kitchen table.

"Sister, I'm not here to argue with you. I want the best for my friend, and I want you to be happy. But you will not find happiness going to a church where you're not wanted."

"I'll talk to you later." Sister Clay hung up the phone.

"My God, bless my friend and please guide her, for she knows not what she is doing." Sister Green stood up and walked to her bedroom to lie down. She was exhausted after talking to Sister Clay. Her friend was a piece of work; and if she didn't stop doing the devil's business, she was going to find herself burning in a pit of fire.

Chapter Twenty-Eight

Soon as Deaconess Perkins arrived at Stephanie's house she immediately took charge. First, the girl needed to eat. She was too skinny. After sitting with Stephanie and getting her comfortable in her room, she went straight to the kitchen. She opened the kitchen cabinets and looked for something to cook. She grabbed two cans of string beans and some rice. Next, she opened the refrigerator and saw some frozen salmon. She decided to cook that, since folks said that was her specialty. She would be there for a few days and would do what she could to put some meat on her bones. She prepared the food and cleaned and dusted. The house was clean, but she knew the young lady had been in the hospital, so she wanted to tidy things up for her.

Stephanie laid in the bed, thinking. She was in love with the pastor. She always had feelings for him, but now they were deep. Not wanting to get hurt again, she held her deepest feelings to herself. The only way the good pastor would find out about her deep love, would be for him to determine them in the passion of her kisses. She touched her lips and reminisced. Just then, her cell rang. It was him. She picked the phone up and answered.

"Hello, Daniel." Stephanie shifted her body in the bed.

"I was calling to check on you. I wanted to stop by for a minute. Are you up for a visit?"

"Sure. Come on over." She lifted her body off the bed and rubbed the sleep from her eyes.

"I'll see you in about forty-five minutes." He stood up, stretched, and looked at his watch.

"Okay. Bye." She jumped up and found something to slip on. She smelled the scent of the food cooking and touched her belly. It was rumbling. She went and took a shower, and when she walked out of her bedroom, she heard Pastor talking to Deaconess Perkins. When she walked into the room, Pastor Winston stood up and walked over to her and gave her a gentle hug. Then, he kissed her cheek.

"Stephanie, I cooked enough food, do you mind if the pastor stays for dinner?" Deaconess Perkins hoped she wasn't viewed as overbearing or trying to take over, but a blind man could see the affection between the two.

"Sure, Daniel. You're welcome to stay. As a matter-of-fact, the aroma of the food smells pretty good up in here. I even smell lemon pound cake, which is one of my favorites."

"Well, wash your hands, people, and come and eat. I love cooking."

They went into the guest bathroom and washed their hands. Pastor Winston guided Stephanie back to the kitchen area with his hand resting on her back.

As they sat down at the table, the pastor offered grace, and they passed the serving dishes and enjoyed the meal. "Thank you, Deaconess Perkins, for coming and staying with me. I appreciate all that you have done."

"Sweetheart, you're welcome. I don't mind helping. I hate what you went through and whatever I can do to help you, I don't mind." Deaconess Perkins took a spoonful of rice and ate it.

"The salmon is delicious. Wow, this is the best I've tasted." He winked at Stephanie.

"Thank you, Pastor. You're so kind." Deaconess smiled, noticing the atmosphere between Pastor Winston and Stephanie.

They talked about current events and what was happening in many of the black communities. "I'm saddened by all the black-on-black crime. I feel helpless because nothing we are doing is working."

Stephanie picked up her glass and took a sip of her cold tea. When she put the glass on the table, it shook the table because of the force of her setting it down. "Sorry, I didn't mean to do that. I guess I get a little frustrated about this topic."

"We all do. It seems like all of our young men are being killed, and now they are taking the women with them." Deaconess Perkins continued to eat.

"Yes, things are dismal at best, but we can rest assured that nothing is too big for God. We must stay faithful and keep praying. We need to get out more and talk to these young people and offer them jobs; maybe that would help." Picking up his napkin and wiping his mouth, he asked Deaconess Perkins to pass the rice.

"Here you go, Pastor. This problem is going to take a lot, but one thing is for sure, we must do something fast because this issue is getting worse."

Everyone agreed and finished eating. After cleaning the table and washing the dishes, they all retreated to the living room. Stephanie turned the television on. "Do you all mind? The news is about to come on."

They sat on the couch and watched the dreaded news. Stephanie was sitting next to the pastor when the news reporter stated that a known rapist was shot down in cold blood the day before and that he was identified as Jimmy Taylor. The newscaster reported he was talking to a woman in a Jeep and someone, either from the car, or out of it, shot him in the head. An investigation is being handled by the drug task force.

Stephanie's body shook with anger, frustration, and pain when she saw his face. "That's him. He's the man who tried to rape me." She laid her head in her open hands and cried.

Deaconess Perkins stood up and excused herself from the living room. She thought it best the pastor handle this situation.

Scooting closer to her he assured, "Stephanie, he's gone now. He can't hurt you anymore." He put his arms around her shoulders and pulled her into his chest.

"Right, Daniel, I know he can't hurt me anymore."

He prayed over Stephanie, while he held her and then he prayed for Jimmy.

"Thank you, Daniel. Really, I'm okay now."

"I'm here for you. God protected you, and He will continue to do so." He squeezed her shoulders lightly. "Stephanie, God brought you through the storm. Remember, there is no water God cannot calm. He's here for you."

"Thank you so much." She reached up and kissed him.

Chapter Twenty-Nine

*T*abitha spent all morning calling Donnie. She was irritated that she was being ignored. Being unnoticed much of her life, except for when she was on a stripper pole, or on one of her mother's boyfriends - who were trying to rape her, she just didn't like it. She would not accept the man she loved playing with her emotions by having regular sex with her and then dropping her. Nah that was a big no-no.

She picked up her phone and called Donnie again. When he didn't answer, she grabbed the cup she was drinking out of, off the table and threw it against the wall. The mug shattered and the pieces flew through the living room. She didn't care. The pain in her heart was so deep. She wanted to hurt someone. Reaching for her phone, she called Stephanie.

"I need to speak to Donnie, Stephanie. I know he's there." Her voice was laced with hate.

"Tabitha, please don't call my number again. Apparently, you didn't get the memo. Donnie and I are not together. He had an affair with you, and I dumped him."

"That's what you say. But every chance he gets, he sneaks back over, and you allow it."

Lifting up from her desk, she said, "Please, girl, don't call me anymore. I don't give a darn about you and Donnie. Please, no more calls. Stay away from me before someone gets hurt."

"You got that right. Your butt is mine." Tabitha ended the call. This was the last time Stephanie would disrespect her. Sweat beads popped out on her forehead, and the hair on her skin rose. She was hot and cold, as chill bumps graced her arms. "Someone is going to pay for my pain, and it's not me."

Tabitha tried to call Donnie again. The phone just rang. Then, the voicemail came on saying his voicemail was full. She jumped off the couch and grabbed her purse and keys. She was going to find that man and get him straight.

****

Pastor Winston stood in his church's conference room talking to his friend and elder. They had spent most of the morning chatting. "I'm happy Stephanie doesn't have to live in fear worrying about that guy coming after her."

"I know that's right. We all know God is able, but some of these people have the spirit of evil wrapped so tightly around their hearts, you have to stay prayed up to prevent sin from entering your house. That man got what he had coming to him." Elder Brown shook his head. "Boy, that's a bad way to go out of this world though."

"Actually, it's not. He didn't see it coming. The news reported that he was shot in the head from the back. I'm so glad God protected Stephanie. Things could be much worse. But thank God, she is okay. Tears dry up, but mental pain stays."

"That was so traumatic for her, after everything she's been through." Elder Brown tapped the cherry wood table in frustration.

"But God, in His wonder, brought her over. I spoke to her this morning and she said she is doing great."

Pushing his chair out from the table to stretch out his legs, "So you and the sister are serious?"

"Well, I'm serious about her. She knows it through my actions. But I'm sure she is taking her time to be sure."

"Is that your wife, Pastor?"

"Yeah, it is... If I do say so myself. I just hope God and Stephanie agree."

"Does she indicate in any way she is reciprocating your feelings?" He lifted his eyebrows waiting for a response.

"Yes. When I kiss her, I feel her love for me. But has she said the words? No. It's been over five months, and she has yet to utter the words I want to hear." Pastor Winston stood up and walked over to the big, picture window and looked out. "Man, it's a beautiful day."

Elder Brown walked over and looked out the window. "Have you told her you love her?"

"Yes, I believe after kissing her, I have said it a couple of times. Don't get me wrong, if kisses could talk, I'd know she loves me."

"So, what are you going to do?"

"I'm inviting her to the conference next month. I want her to see my world… To see what happens and to know her position with me. I want her to attend and get to know me, the church folks so that she will understand how she fits in this lifestyle."

"Well, let's just pray it don't run her away. Some of these Christian women can be vicious; especially, when they want a handsome, young pastor all to themselves. Stephanie needs to see the way women gloat over you so she can learn how to handle things as a first lady."

"I believe she can handle it." He rubbed his hands together. "I have no doubt she would do well as my first lady."

"Well, in all respect, Pastor, you are a good man of God. In all the years of your assignment as our preacher, you have been faithful to God and have not abused your power of trust and guidance. I can't say that about many men of God - including myself." Elder Brown returned to the conference table and sat back down. "You take her to that conference and introduce her to your world."

"I plan to do that." He cleared off his desk and asked, "Anything you need me to do before I leave?"

"Not really. Tomorrow, we'll need to visit two members who are sick and shut-in. Also, don't forget you have a baptismal coming up this Sabbath."

"Thanks for keeping me informed. There are 20 more people ready for baptism. God is good. I'm going to run some errands, and if you need me, you know how to reach me."

"Alright, Pastor. I'll check in later." He stood up and walked over and shook the pastor's hand.

"See you later, Elder."

Chapter Thirty

*D*onnie sat and sulked over Stephanie. He picked up the phone and called Kent's grandmother and asked if he could pick the boy up. She agreed. Then, he called Jasper's foster mom and asked the same. She encouraged Donnie to come pick him up because he had been released from juvenile detention and needed some encouragement. She also informed his mentor that he hung out too much with gang members.

Donnie promised to help the young man and to talk to him about it. He hung up the phone, got dressed, and left. He picked Jasper up first so that he could spend some time alone with him. When he pulled up to the house, he observed Jasper sitting on the porch with some older boys who held beer cans in their hands and cursed like drunken sailors.

"Hey, Jasper. What's happening, man?" He strolled to the porch and gave Jasper a fist bump. "What's up, fellas?"

"Nothing, man," one young man said without passion or interest. They turned back to each other, laughing and cussing.

"You guys think you can respect me?"

"Sorry, dude," one muttered, as they all stood up and started walking away.

"So, how are you all doing in school?" Donnie propped his leg on the bottom step and caused them to stop and turn to face him.

"School is for punks," the young guy holding the malt liquor, beer can said with his lips all twisted into a negative-looking circle.

"Oh, you don't say? You all standing here drinking and cursing and not going to school, how does that help your future?"

"Future? Man, we don't live past the age of twenty-five," one of the teens responded.

The teens gave each other fist bumps and laughed. The question made them giggle, but their responses spoke of sadness.

"You all don't need to feel so hopeless. You can live, if you change your mindset, go to school, and consider some positive activities." Donnie wanted to save them. He wanted to change their way of thinking, make them long and desire for change. "Don't you realize with work you can achieve so much? You can make it. Please don't be idle and lie and wait for death. You can go to school, graduate, work, and be married." He didn't finish speaking because one of the young guys interrupted with an exasperated sigh.

"Sorry, man, those dreams don't happen in the hood," another young man said.

"Anything is possible anywhere. Where do you think I came from, anyway? You just got to want it."

"We all about fam in this hood. We watch out for each other. That's the hood," the first guy responded. "We do what we can to survive."

"Nothing's wrong with escaping, but if you want to live and think past surviving for a day, you have to plan to survive for a lifetime."

Donnie hated to meet so many hopeless teenagers. He just wanted them to understand that they could do so much if they aspired to. But he realized he couldn't reach them. Even Jasper lacked concern. He just stood idly by as he watched, not responding and participating in the conversation. He just looked bored. "Hey, what if I offered you all an opportunity to change your life? To enroll back in school and to graduate and go to college?"

The second teen stood up and dusted his pants off and said, "Ain't nobody about that life. I make more money slinging dope than I would on a job. I'm my boss. I do what I want to."

"So, you accept that with selling dope your choices are limited to three things: death, hospital, or jail? Those are some pretty unattractive benefits with your slinging drugs job."

"Like we said, we don't live past the age of twenty-five, so who cares?" the third guy jumped in.

Before Donnie could continue, the first young man said, "Let's roll up outta here."

They all stood up, gave Jasper a fist bump, and left without saying another word to Donnie.

Donnie looked at Jasper and said, "There's better choices, son. You follow me?"

"That's what you say, Mr. Donnie. I hope so. I'm trying, but my background says nothing good will happen for me." He brushed his thick, brown hand across his head and stood up. "People like me never win. The cards never fall in our direction."

"Come on, son. Remove that negative mindset out of your head. You can do and become anything you want, but like with everything else, if you simply put in the work the rewards will be forthcoming. Even messing with gangs is work. Nothing is easy."

"Yeah right. But I got this." Jasper walked to Donnie's car. "I don't need your help on this, I got this."

"You don't have anything. But remember, I'm here for you. Just pick up the phone and call me. Desire for better."

"I appreciate that. I recognize your love for me. Thanks, but my boys got my back too. Don't worry." He opened the door and jumped into the front seat of Donnie's black Mercedes.

Donnie rolled his eyes and said, "Lord, help me to help this kid." He pulled the door open, got in, started the ignition, and went to pick up Kent.

They picked Kent up and Donnie took them for pizza and to the art museum.

"Hey, Donnie, the art gallery sucks." Jasper hunched his shoulders up, as they walked around observing the exhibits and said, "This is boring."

"Art is educational. It affects all areas of our lives from social, emotional, and even academic achievement. People who understand art and music do better in reading and math, and it helps to build critical thinking skills, as well as strengthening your concentration and building your confidence."

Jasper laughed. "Art don't do all that." He laughed again.

"Boy, I'm trying to expose you to some good things in life. That stuff you think is important, like those Jordans, and all that other mess, has nothing on developing your mind." He put his arm around Jasper's shoulders. "Try, man. Do better. Reach higher."

"Okay, Donnie. I'll do better." He gave Donnie a huge smile. "So, what's that picture on that wall?"

Chapter Thirty-One

astor Winston picked up his phone to call Stephanie. When she answered, she said, "Hey, Daniel. How are you?"

He could feel her smile coming through the phone line. Her voice perked up and presented an up tempo, musical pitch, while the tone emphasized a soft, high and exciting sound. That's what he loved about her. She always seemed so happy, even with all the problems and struggles she'd been through during her lifetime.

"Hey, sweetheart. What's on your schedule today?" He blushed when he said the word sweetheart. It came easy for him.

The smile on her face increased in width at the sound of the word sweetheart. She answered, "I'm headed to the office. Once I finish there, I'm going home. What are you doing?"

"Waiting on you to come through." He changed the phone to his left hand.

"I can come by around four. Is that good?"

"Sure, baby. I'll prepare dinner." He shoved his left hand into his pocket. His heartbeat raced at the words coming from his mouth.

"Ok. Then I'll meet you this evening. Talk to you soon." She hit end on her cellphone. She tapped it again to make certain the phone hung up. Then, she grabbed her cell and called her best friend.

"Regina, girl, when are you coming back home? You stay in Los Angeles. I miss you."

"I miss you too, sis. But this case I'm working on is taking forever. I will be there next week." Regina laughed. "So, what's my best friend been up too?"

"Girl, trying to make it. That's all. But I do want to share some news with you."

Regina screamed. "You're getting married?"

"Girl, hush. One day I am, but not now." Stephanie whistled. "You need to stop."

"I'm serious. What has it been? Almost seven months, and you and the pastor are not engaged?" She blew air into the phone. "A blind man can view you two are in love."

"Girl, that's not what I wanted to talk about today. I wanted to tell you that they found the guy who jumped me."

"Are you serious?" She released the breath she held in. "When did that happen? How?"

"Girl, someone shot him in the head and left him in the middle of the street. That's how they found him, then I contacted the police department and told them that he was the person who tried to rape me. I remembered him as soon as I spotted his face on the news."

The ladies continued to talk, and she told her about Deaconess Perkins coming to stay with her and how the pastor took care of her during the entire incident. "He's been my rock."

"Do you love him?" Regina asked.

"With everything in me." Stephanie touched her heart. "I'm going to be with him this evening."

"Hang in there, girl. I think God has led you to the one. Another thing, karma is something else. That guy sought to harm you and look how things ended for him. What happened is sad, but you can't hurt others and think you won't suffer in the end."

"I would never wish death on anyone. But I will say, I rest comfortable and allowed Deaconess Perkins to go home. Knowing he cannot hurt me gives me peace."

"Well, we'll talk about everything next week. I'm looking forward to seeing you. I'm happy for you, sister."

"Before you hang up, have you met anyone yet?" Stephanie waited for the response.

"Yeah, I met this guy, but I will tell you more about him. He's an attorney and he's single, good-looking and works in Los Angeles, but we'll talk soon. I'm scheduled back in the courtroom.

"Okay. We'll talk soon." They both expressed their love for each other and ended the call.

Stephanie finished running her errands and arrived at Pastor Winston's home right at 4:00 p.m. After she parked and got out of the car in his circular driveway, she walked up to the door and rang the doorbell. He answered and pulled her into the foyer. He looked her deeply into her eyes and gave her a passionate kiss that weakened her legs. She held on to him for dear life.

They walked into the living room, and she inhaled the scent of the teriyaki aroma permeating through the house. "Is that chicken teriyaki?"

"Yes, it is. I cooked it for us." He gloated.

"You can cook like that?" She touched him teasingly in his chest.

"With you, I can do anything. He took her by the arm and led her into the kitchen so he could check on his food. The smell enticed him to pick up a fork, and he scooped up some and offered it to her. She took a mouthful.

"Mmm… that's so good."

He set the pots on the stove at a warm temperature, and then he escorted her into the great room.

"Sit down, I need to talk to you." He went to the table and picked up some pamphlets. "In two weeks, I am going to a five-day conference. I'm preaching and speaking on some panels, and I want you to go as my guest." He handed the pamphlets to her.

Stephanie looked through the materials. She looked at him. "What does this mean?" Tears welled up in her eyes.

"Well, we've been spending a lot of time together. I care for you deeply. I want you to understand what I do." He sat down next to her on the dark brown, leather couch.

"I understand your world."

He picked up her right hand and kissed the back of it. "Not like you need to."

"You mean, like the women who flock around you? I witnessed that."

"That's not all. The time I put into my ministry. The preaching, teaching, visiting, studying. I want you entrenched in this so that you won't worry or doubt me."

"Okay. I understand. I'll go, but we're getting separate rooms."

"I'm celibate, and I wouldn't ask you to sleep with me without the benefit of marriage. The old me might, but not the saved me." He smiled and kissed her cheek. Then he stood up and reached into his back pocket and pulled his wallet out and a card. "Here, take this card and buy you some things."

"Daniel, we're better than that. I don't need your money." She stood up to face him.

"There are two, major, ballroom parties we are attending, and since I invited you to join me, please allow me to pay for the dresses and shoes you'll need."

"Daniel, I cannot take your money. That's not my character."

"I understand. But really, I want to do this. Please let me." He poked his lips out and gave her the saddest puppy eyes.

"Ok. I will do this as long as you grasp that I'm not reciprocating with sex."

He chuckled. "Not now, but one day. But let's make it through this conference and note what you think." He kissed her again. "Let's eat. I'm starving." He took her hand and walked through the house, and she stopped to wash her hands. He did the same. He kissed her again. "Thank you."

"For what?" She smiled while gazing at him.

"For spending time with me."

"That's so easy for me to do. I enjoy being in your presence. You amaze me." She kissed his cheek.

Pastor Winston couldn't contain the joy leaping across his face as he smiled. The smile spread so wide, it tickled his cheeks, as it stretched from one end to the next. Thankful and happy, he whispered to God, "Thank You."

Chapter Thirty-Two

Stephanie went shopping and bought two dresses and two pairs of shoes. She tried to be reasonable, but she wanted to look extra special for Daniel and others. This would be her first time attending a large church conference, and she didn't comprehend what to expect. She grasped women would swoon over Daniel, she expected that. A handsome man who looked even better than Morris Chestnut, an actor, would for sure draw attention. Still, she didn't fear competition, but lately, women started to become vicious. That bothered her.

One Saturday at church, two women cornered her in the bathroom, wanting her to explain her relationship with the pastor and asked her all sorts of questions. She ignored them until one backed her into a corner and threatened her, but Deaconess Perkins and another deaconess entered the ladies room and ran the women off.

She experienced women's capabilities, but if she wanted to make a life with the pastor, she had to understand what the expectation of him was and learn to handle her role as his lady.

She shopped at Frontenac and went to Neiman Marcus, where she found a white Jovani dress, with one shoulder, ruffled-trim, mermaid gown and a Theia, cold-shoulder, and open back, black dress. Then she purchased two pairs of Christian Louboutin shoes to set the dresses off. She thought long and hard about spending nearly four thousand dollars on the items. But it occurred to her that he recognized her taste and the designers she wore, which is why he probably offered his card. Still though, she didn't want to disappoint him, so she decided to pay for the dresses and shoes herself. She refused to use his card. He wouldn't be disappointed. One thing about it, she would represent him in the highest, classiest way she could.

Stephanie looked forward to the conference and decided to call her mom to ask for more information, so she could be on her best behavior. Her parents spent months traveling. They delighted in their senior citizen status and wanted to view the world while their health remained good. They had a habit of popping in and out of town. This week they were in town.

Stephanie contacted her mom from the restaurant and gave her the arrival time for her visit. Her mom stated how happy the sound of her daughter's voice made her. She missed her daughter and couldn't wait to give her the gifts she purchased for her.

Stephanie stopped at Talayna's to satisfy the desire for lasagna. She decided to dine in. While eating, her cellphone rang and she answered it quietly.

"Hey, Daniel."

"Hi, sweetheart. How's your day going?"

"All is well," she whispered. "I'm in a restaurant eating, which is why I'm whispering."

"Did you find something to wear?"

"Yeah, I found two evening gowns and two pairs of shoes. I think you will be impressed." She decided not to tell him she didn't use his card.

"I'm happy you're going with me. The flight arrangements and hotel reservations are scheduled."

"I'm excited. My first Christian conference. This is new to me." She looked around to check for ear hustlers, who lingered, trying to listen to her conversation.

"You're in for a treat. I have Bible study today at noon and seven p.m. If you need me, text me."

"I do have a question, and you may think I'm silly."

"No questions you ask me are silly, nor are you." He held the phone and hoped he wouldn't be disappointed by something he couldn't deal with.

"Are we seriously dating?" She took a deep breath.

"I don't make it a practice to kiss women on the mouth that I'm not serious about." He laughed.

"Well, you never asked me. I don't want to make any assumptions. You do realize what happens when you assume?"

"Stephanie, would you consider being my one and only"

"Well…" She paused.

"Did I ask correctly?" He held his breath.

"Pastor, you asked correctly, and yes I will be your one and only." She held the phone tightly and chewed on her lip.

A smile crept across his face. Nothing could make him happier than what he experienced at that moment. "Thank you. I will call you later."

Now, Stephanie could release the air out of her lungs, and she was more confident about leaving town for five days with the pastor. This conversation made her experience satisfaction and gave her comfort with the idea of being in Washington, DC with him as his one and only. "Life is good." She dug into her lasagna. "And so is this food."

Chapter Thirty-Three

Something pulled Donnie toward the church. For the past three nights, there was a strong tug for him to take the boys to church. He didn't understand it. On several occasions, he attended his mother's church with Stephanie and enjoyed the preaching, but he hadn't been anywhere near one after the breakup. The break up occurred nearly eight months ago, and still, his heart longed for her. He decided to wake up Saturday, bright and early, pick up the boys and go to his mom's church.

Kent, Jasper, and Donnie arrived at the New Salem Adventist Church at 11:00 a.m. Divine Services began at 11:01. The choir voices rang throughout the sanctuary, and the congregation stood and joined in as the pastor and the pulpit speakers marched through the middle aisle to reach the platform. As a child, his grandmother sang, "When We All Get to Heaven," all the time. As he listened to the words, it brought back warm memories.

They sat next to Donnie's mom. Kent pulled on Donnie's leg. "I can't see." His short stature served at a disadvantage for the young boy. Donnie picked him up so he could view the singers in the choir stand. Kent clapped his hands but Jasper held a somber face. He didn't want to come to church. He didn't even know God.

The pastor offered a prayer. "Dear God, we are here today to serve You. Please bless the speakers on today so that someone might receive a Word from on high, and open the door for someone who doesn't have a relationship with You that they will get a mighty good introduction to Your Word. Lord, people are struggling. They're dying without an opportunity to experience a loving God who, when asked, will do for them like no other. This God is so powerful, so loving, that even when we don't ask Him - because we don't know Him - He still loves us so much that He works behind the scene, making sure our needs are met. Thank You for this day, Your love, and for sending Your Son to die for us and save us from sin. In the name of Jesus, we pray. Amen."

The pastor asked everyone to be seated, and they proceeded with the order of the program. Jasper pulled out his cellphone and attempted to play games.

"Put that away and pay attention," Donnie demanded.

He put it away and listened to the pastor. The pastor spoke about Unfair Grace. He preached on how you have to yield to God for yourself. And how you cannot rely on anyone else's knowledge; not your relatives, husbands, friends, church members, but lean on Him. "We must live worshiping God." The pastor said.

He also spoke about having patience, and that God makes promises to us that He keeps. He was talking about repentance and developing a relationship with God. The pastor state, "When God tells us to do something, He is using us. He wants us to tell people His messages. He gives us assignments." Donnie listened eagerly.

As the pastor spoke, it occurred to Donnie that God had spoken directly to his appearance at church. He thanked God for opening his heart and mind to receive his call. Just sitting in the pews and listening to the pastor's sermon gave him peace. He believed God called him and He requested him to stop running. He didn't want to run anymore. He wanted peace. He wanted the storms to blow over in his life. He heard the pastor say not to hate the storm, but to dissect it and understand His assignments. He wanted to stop and give his heart to the Lord and to save Jasper and Kent. He looked over at Kent and Jasper and realized they had their ears wide open as they listened intently. He said under his breath, "Lord, help these young boys to survive and give me the strength and words to help them."

Donnie thanked God for inspiring him to visit the church, and he planned to come back again the following week. He kissed his mother and left.

****

Pastor Winston put out a call to Stephanie to establish if she'd finished dressing so they could leave for brunch and then to the keynote session. Her phone rang.

"Good Morning, Daniel." Her chirpy voice pleased his ears.

"Are you ready to go down to the conference?"

"I'm already down in the lobby. I'm waiting on you."

"I'm on my way down." They hung up. He became a little jealous because she left him but shook it off. He invited Stephanie to learn about his life, his calling, and should not expect her to be all under him, even though he wanted her to be. "Lord, I know Your children. Some are still dealing with sin, please help me to be a blessing to someone and help me to handle those who will overstep their boundaries with Stephanie." He prayed and thanked God for all his future blessings.

As soon as he arrived in the lobby, he saw Stephanie. She looked like an angel, surrounded by four pastors. That is why he prayed. He knew that sin even happened among those who were trying to serve God, and he understood that God still cleaned and worked on broken people.

Stephanie wore a bandage, white dress that fit her body like a glove. She also had on some stilettos - white red bottoms. She looked good. Her hair hung around her shoulders, and her good looks had people staring at her with envy and interest.

She talked with confidence to the pastors, and they flirted and hosted greedy smiles on their faces. When she saw Daniel staring, she smiled and excused herself from the group. When she walked away, their thirsty eyes followed.

Walking over to him, she spoke. "Good morning, Daniel."

He reached over and kissed her lips quickly. "Good morning. You look beautiful."

A smile lingered on her face. "Thank you, and you look handsome."

His chest poked out while he reached up and rested his hand on the small of her back and escorted her into the ballroom. They found a table and sat down. At the table sat Pastor James Davis and his wife, Denise. Pastor Winston introduced everyone, and Denise and Stephanie took to each other quickly.

They laughed and talked and seemed genuinely happy to have met each other. They lived in the same area. The pleasure in Daniel's heart deepened to witness two women he respected get along.

Denise's heart was cradled in goodness. She was a newlywed who others tested and tried to break her spirit before and since marrying the handsome Pastor Davis. Her strength, with the will of God, prevailed. She and Stephanie would make good friends.

"How's everything going for you, Stephanie?" Denise inquired.

"Things are great. I'm looking forward to this conference. This is my first time. As a matter-of-fact, this is new to me." She picked up her water and took a sip.

"Well, this conference is my second one. But is this your first time dating a pastor?"

Stephanie smiled and took her time responding.

"Sorry for being so forward. I guess you're seeing each other. It's written all over your faces, and nothing is wrong with that." She touched her shoulder as a sign of caring.

"I've never dated a pastor. This is different for me. I suppose dating him is like dating any man though." She buttered her roll.

"That's where you're wrong. He's a man, but to some women, he's a rock star for Jesus."

Laughing, Stephanie said, "Denise, please say that again. Did I catch that correctly?"

"Yes, you did. Women perceive them as special. Rock stars. Close to God. But honestly, there is nothing wrong with it, except they are not God. They have families, they fall in love, and their spouses want respect. But some people consider their spouses as people in the way. Everybody is not disrespectful, but you'll have to learn how to deal with all types of people and be the helpmate your husband needs." Denise smiled, picked at her fruit, and took a forkful.

"Well, I'm not married to him."

"Yet, girl. Not yet." They continued to talk, and every few minutes Pastor Winston would turn to check on her.

Smiling and glowing, Pastor Davis asked, "Stephanie, are you ok?"

"Yes. Everything is fine."

As they all chatted, two more couples came to the table to join them, and Pastor Davis introduced everyone. Stephanie was pleased because Daniel had no problems expressing his feelings and letting people know that his heart belonged to her. She was proud and scared at the same time. But she knew she loved him, and learning about God, his life, and how to be a good helpmate was what she planned to do – with God's help.

Chapter Thirty-Four

Tabitha had lost her mind. She didn't understand what was happening to her. She had begun to stalk Donnie. She showed up on his job and caused problems, and now she found herself parked in front of his house. She rubbed her stomach. "Daddy is going to be with us," she said to her belly as she caressed it.

Tabitha pulled out her notebook and wrote down some notes. She decided to decode a conversation she previously had with him. She wrote down that he loved her and wanted to marry her and raise their child together. She ignored the fact that he told her to leave him alone and gave her money for an abortion. Even though she heard those words out of his mouth, they meant nothing to her. She knew he spoke in codes because he didn't want others to know what they discussed when together. The truth about their relationship resided in the pages of her journal.

Picking up the phone, she called him again. But the phone went to voicemail. She picked up her journal and jotted down that he wouldn't answer the phone because the FBI (Federal Bureau of Investigations) spent the bulk of their time eavesdropping and they had to be careful. Too many people spied on them, and so they had to be cautious and discreet. In the meantime, she called Stephanie.

When Stephanie didn't answer, she noted in her journal that again she stood in the way, and then Tabitha searched the yard for Donnie, which just made her angry. She was sick and tired of Stephanie coming after her man, and if she didn't stop, Tabitha moaned,

"I'm going to take care of her as well."

****

Donnie's perplexity deepened. He shifted his body next to the window and peeked out. Tabitha sat in her car watching his home. She had been there for hours. At first, she showed up at his job and tried to break into his office. When his secretary called the police, she ran out, accusing the secretary of sabotaging her marriage with Donnie.

The lady spiraled out of control. Donnie thought about the first time he met her at a bar. She dressed nicely and had a sweet personality. He asked her to dance and she agreed. They danced the night away. They talked, and she demonstrated she was a great people person and conversationalist. She seemed to have it so together. Tabitha was white, and he had never dated outside of his race, so this intrigued him. He didn't love her. He had sought fun before he settled down.

He had been sleeping with Tabitha for months, when Stephanie found out. Now he regretted having an affair on the only woman he truly loved. It seemed that he had lost her forever. It had been some time ago when she found him in bed sexing another woman. When she ran out of the bedroom, leaving him bleeding from the head and Tabitha sliding down a wall scared of being killed, he had not been able to reel her back.

He continued to watch her. Tabitha was crouched down in the car talking. It seemed she held an intense conversation with someone, but he didn't see anyone in the car with her and his cellphone kept ringing. When he looked at the number on his phone, just like the one before, her name popped up. Donnie didn't answer her continuous calls to him. This had to stop before someone got hurt. He decided to call the police.

After he had made the call, Tabitha came on the porch and started peeking through his windows. He opened the front side window and spoke loudly, "Tabitha, I called the police, and they are on their way. You are going to have to pay a hefty fee to get out of jail."

"Hey, baby. Answer the door. We need to talk about our relationship." She smiled and batted her eyes at him.

"Do you have money to get out of jail? If not, I suggest you step out of my yard and life." He pulled his window closed and walked away.

"You know you love us, Donnie. Don't you walk away from us." She banged her open hand on the top windowpane. "Open the door, I promise to be good."

Tears flowed from her eyes, as her body bloated with rage. *How could he disrespect his child and me?* She swiped the tears dropping down her face. The anger inside her swelled and progressed quickly to hate toward the love of her life. She didn't have any money to pay for jail costs, so she jumped off the porch and jogged to her car. Just when she turned the car on, a police cruiser turned down the street. She pulled off and left, vowing to make Donnie pay for causing all this drama.

Chapter Thirty-Five

Stephanie was mesmerized by Pastor Winston speaking. She couldn't take her eyes off him. He was an eloquent speaker and had the attention of everyone glued to him. He was discussing how much God loves us. His mannerisms expressed confidence and knowledge. Stephanie was so proud to be his lady.

While he was speaking at the podium, Denise whispered to her, "He's a great speaker and has a big fan base."

"A fan base?" She looked from Denise to Pastor Winston and back to the audience. She immediately noticed women smiling at him and trying to secure his attention.

"That's right, Pastor. Preach." Then the women would call his name, as if they were in the Spirit and stand up without smoothing or pulling their dresses down. Several women looked over at her and rolled their eyes.

"Oh God," Stephanie moaned.

"Sister, it's going to be alright. Just stay in prayer and let God lead your life."

Later that evening, the two couples went out to dinner and took a tour through Washington D.C. Although both Denise and Stephanie had visited the area many times through their nonprofit businesses, they were having fun with their men.

After the tour and dinner, Stephanie and Daniel went to the lobby to talk, while Pastor Davis and Denise went to their room. Daniel was not ready to end the night. He had a beautiful date and enjoyed being with her. Stephanie had changed into a red maxi dress and some silver and red flat sandals, to be comfortable while on the tour. It seemed no matter what she wore, she was stunning.

They held hands and talked. There were times their eyes did the talking and they allowed it to happen. "How was your first day of conference?" Pastor Daniel wanted to hear what she had to say.

"I've had a beautiful day. It was more than I expected."

"I'm glad to hear that."

"Your sermon was very informative and inspiring. Did you always want to preach?"

"No. It never occurred to me. I was living in the fast lane, enjoying life. I had no cares or concerns because I was doing well and making a lot of money. But God had other plans."

He told her about Pamela and how God had called him. She was surprised. He had an interesting life, and like her, he had lost his first love. They shared that kind of pain, but she believed his was even worse because Pamela was gone from the earth.

She listened to him and held his hand. He told her so much about his life, and she thanked him for confiding in her. As they continued to talk, her heart grew fonder of him. She asked him to pray with her and they prayed that God would watch over them both and protect their love.

While sitting on the couch, a group of women came into the lobby. They were loud and dressed as if they had been out to a club. They saw the couple and noticed the handsome pastor. Immediately, they sauntered over to talk to him.

Disrespecting Stephanie, one lady dressed in a gold dress started talking to the pastor. "Good evening, good-looking." She didn't wait for him to respond. "Heard your sermon this morning and it was so darn good. As a matter-of-fact, I can't wait to see you preach again. My name is Champagne." She stumbled toward him.

"Excuse me, Champagne, this is Stephanie."

"I didn't ask about her. I'm talking to you." Her words slurred together.

The pastor stood up and helped Stephanie off the couch. "Sorry, but please excuse us."

"That's all you got to say?" Her friends started laughing and giving each other high fives. "You just gon' walk away with your fine self?"

Pastor Winston held Stephanie's hand tightly inside of his. They left the area quickly, without conversation. Once outside in the fresh air, they both giggled. Stephanie was the first to speak.

"You handled that well. I'm proud of you." She wrapped her arms around his waist. "That couldn't have been easy."

"Well, sometimes when you can't say something nice, you don't say anything at all. I didn't want to instigate that into something more. Those women had been drinking. This is why I said that sometimes people mean well, and they are struggling Christians, straddling the line between Jesus and Satan. They may not think anything is wrong with what they did. But when you are saved, it's like a light shining over your head. The Bible says in Matthew 7:20: 'Wherefore by their fruits ye shall know them.' There is no need to make matters worse. Truly, you cannot talk to a person who has been drinking and bent on giving you a hard time."

Stephanie kissed him. She was so in love with him. They walked back into the hotel and retired to their separate rooms.

Chapter Thirty-Six

The conference was going well. Stephanie was up front and center watching women fawn over Daniel. She thought about it; if she were single and met him, she would probably try to hit on him too. However, she realized that her character was different and she was always taught to allow the man to seek her out. But still, she didn't fault the women for wanting Pastor Winston because he was handsome, a man of God, and he had a good heart. What she didn't like was the disrespect shown to her and him.

For instance, when she was in the restroom, a young sister bumped into her hard, knocking her over to the trash can. She didn't apologize, even when Stephanie said the words 'excuse you' for her.

The woman looked at her, rolled her eyes and walked out the restroom. Another time, she overheard a conversation in the bathroom between some women saying that Pastor Winston had brought a skank to the conference, and when he finished using her, she would be waiting. When she came out the bathroom stall, they all just laughed, like they had said something funny.

The other thing that happened was several preachers who were hounding her, turned out to be married. Every time Daniel left her side, those philandering preachers couldn't wait to step to her. One had the nerve to ask her to dinner. He told her he was married, but God allowed him to see other women.

Pastor Winston would intervene when he saw it happening, and she believed he'd said something to the pastors. But it didn't matter, they ignored his requests and continued to pursue her.

Overall, the conference was inspirational, and she met many good people. She also developed a real friendship with Denise Davis. They went shopping and to lunch several times. They had so much in common, with their love for people, their nonprofit companies and their love for fashion. She looked forward to seeing her when they returned from the conference.

At the conference, she and Daniel grew closer. She also had an opportunity to meet his parents. Charlotte and Daniel Winston, Sr., were friendly and classy people. They came to the conference on day two. They doted on their son and treated her with the utmost respect. They had dinner and breakfast together and seemed very pleased with his choice. Charlotte invited Stephanie on a shopping trip that evening, and they walked around several malls until they were too tired to walk any place else.

The following day, Daniel, Stephanie, and his parents went on a bus tour. It took them to the Washington Monument, Lincoln Memorial, the White House and other places. It was an excellent tour. Afterward, they all went to Georgetown to do some shopping. They walked on the old, original, cobblestone streets and visited shops that had everything from big labels to small boutiques. They finished off the day eating at a quaint, classic, and elegant place called 1789 Restaurant. Stephanie enjoyed spending time with Daniel and his parents. They were both college professors and were open and fun people. His mom told Stephanie she was beautiful and thought her son had found someone special.

Stephanie was happy. When she walked, there was a pep in her step. She had spent three days at the conference and this night was one of the balls. She decided to wear the white gown she bought from Neiman. She showered, dressed, and had a makeup artist and hair stylist come to her room to help her dress. She wanted to look fabulous, and chose a makeup artist who specialized in the natural look because she didn't need too much on. She wanted Daniel to be proud to have her on his arm.

He arrived at her door, which was down the hall from his room, at 6:30 p.m. When she opened the door, his mouth fell open and he proclaimed, "Sweetheart, you are stunning." He was wearing a white suit with a black and white tie and a black shirt. His shoes were black, and his custom cufflinks were silver with white diamonds.

Stephanie wanted to pull him into her bedroom and never leave, but she knew that wouldn't please God. Instead, she walked into his arms and gave him a kiss that was so passionate that he picked her up, breaking the kiss. She stared down at him from the air. "Baby, don't kiss me like that. You're breaking me down." He put her back on the floor. She grabbed his right arm and rubbed his muscles.

"My man is strong."

"But that move just weakened me. That kiss was something else." He bent down and gently kissed her neck.

"We better go before we find ourselves in trouble."

Pastor Winston practically drug her out of the hotel room. "Don't be scared. I don't bite," Stephanie teased.

"Baby, I want you to, which is why I am pulling you to the elevator. I don't want us in any trouble." He tilted her head up and looked into her eyes. "You make me happy."

Smiling, Stephanie responded, "You do the same for me."

They entered the hotel lobby and saw so many beautiful couples and people milling around, laughing and checking each other out. Everyone was looking nice, and the lobby was flowing with black and white outfits. Pastor Davis and First Lady Denise walked over and hugged the couple. They complimented each other on their looks. Then, they went to find their reserved tables. Pastor Winston and Pastor Davis were both speaking. Over the dinner, there was much chatter, as an orchestra played soft music.

Pastor Winston went up to the podium and spoke about the Faithful Few. He asked the audience if they were a part of the faithful few Christians, and they resounded with loud ovations. The majority of the room stood up. He gave them some information on how to be a lamp to Christ for others. His sermon was inspirational, yet it also gave people some standards to live as Jesus wanted us to.

Immediately after service there was a special presentation. Pastor Winston was being honored for his work at the national level. He had spent time working with congregations and pastors in seven states training them on handling mental health issues in the church.

Pastor Davis gave some remarks and presented an award for community service to Daniel. When he made his remarks, he thanked his parents, church members who voted, and the conference committee for such a great conference, and then he acknowledged the support of his special friend, Stephanie Whitmore. When he called her name out, almost every head turned and looked at her; most of the people smiled and clapped. Stephanie knew about his work but knew he mentioned her so she wouldn't feel left out.

When Daniel returned to the table, he sat his beautiful plaque down on the table. Stephanie turned it to her and read the inscription. She kissed his cheek and told him she was so proud of him. "Thank you for making me a part of this."

"I wouldn't have had it any other way. Thank you for coming and supporting me." He squeezed her hand.

The rest of the conference went by quickly, and before Stephanie knew it, it was time to go back home. Pastor Winston enjoyed his time at the conference. When he arrived at her room to help her with her luggage, he told her, "I've enjoyed this time with you. Thank you for coming, because I appreciate it. Thank you so much for sharing this time with me. I know it wasn't easy, but you handled this well."

He pulled her into an embrace. "Stephanie, I love you."

She was speechless. Suddenly, her heart leaped out of her chest and into her hand. She didn't know what to do or say. She was scared. It was almost as if someone was attacking her. But this simple admission of love should have made her feel secure, but it nearly scared her to death. He waited, hoping and praying she would say she loved him, but all he heard was her breathing and saw a look of fear in her eyes. He thought, *Lord, did I just lose my heart?*

Chapter Thirty-Seven

*W*hen Stephanie and Daniel arrived home, things went back to normal with their business responsibilities. Although Stephanie never told the pastor she loved him, she showed him with her actions. She was very affectionate to him. She squeezed his hand, hugged his neck, and most of the time, couldn't stop kissing him. She attended church with him as much as she could.

Daniel was so faithful. He fully believed she loved him and that she was the one. He understood she might have been afraid of making a commitment after what she had been through. He was willing to wait. He loved her dearly.

One day while preparing for Bible class, he shared his heart with Elder Brown. They had always been close and he treated him as a brother. They were in his office and planning which elder would visit the sick and shut-in.

Elder Brown asked him how things were going with him and Stephanie. He leaned on the chair in front of Daniel's desk.

"Things are good. I'm happy, and I believe she is too." He flipped open his Bible.

"Are you going to ask her to marry you?" Elder Brown shuffled his feet and pulled the chair back and sat down.

"I plan to. You know, I gave her my credit card so she could purchase some things for the conference. I did that because I asked her to go and I didn't want her to use her money. She didn't spend a dime."

"How did you find out?"

"I got the bill and there was nothing new on it. Apparently, she spent her money." He looked up from the Bible and shook his head. "That made me want her more."

"I understand that...Sister not after your money."

"I mean, I offered the card to her and requested she use it, even though she resisted. She took it to shut me up. But she sure did look great at the galas held at the conference." His dimples in his cheeks deepened.

"You love her. It's a blessing to find someone to love." Elder Brown cupped his hands together. "Everyone needs somebody to love."

"I've been praying, and I know she's the one. I just need her to know." He pushed his chair back and stood up. "It's about time to start Bible class." His phone vibrated in his pocket. He pulled it out and answered it. It was Stephanie.

Hi, Daniel. I thought I would call you to let you know I'm in the parking lot, coming to your class. I decided to come over to the noon class instead of getting lunch today."

"That's great. I was going to call you because I wanted to see if I could pick you up for dinner tonight. I'm grateful you're able to come to noon Bible class today."

"I hope to visit more in the future during this time... Daniel, I have several late meetings today, but I can meet you for dinner tonight," she said, as she opened her car door and locked it.

"How about Tony's in St. Louis?"

"The one on Market?" She strolled to the church, as she spoke into her cell.

"Yes. I have reservations for six-thirty tonight. Elder Brown will handle the seven o'clock Bible class. We had made plans for him to teach the night class several weeks ago."

"Ok. I can do that. I'll be in the church in a minute. See you in a second."

"Well, Elder Brown, I think tonight is the night. Keep us in prayer."

"Pastor, you and Stephanie will do fine. God has this one. Let's rush to class before people start looking for us."

Stephanie entered the church and walked into the ladies' room to freshen up. She was happy she didn't have a meeting to attend because she wanted to spend time at Bible class. She couldn't always make it because she often had book signings to attend in the late evenings. To her surprise, Daniel attended several of her recent signings. But recently, Daniel started hosting noon Bible classes to accommodate congregants who wanted to come during the lunch hour. Her plan was to attend more of the noon classes.

She put on her lipstick and combed her hair. While combing her hair, Sister Jamie Johnson entered the bathroom. She had seen her a few times at services when she had attended.

They talked for a minute until Stephanie left. When she walked into the sanctuary, Pastor Winston was teaching his class. She sat down near the back and tried to concentrate. She was having a hard time trying to follow the lesson. She couldn't seem to focus.

When class was over, Pastor headed straight to her. "Are you okay?"

"Yes. I'm fine. But I have to go back to the office for a minute." She turned to leave, but he pulled her back toward him.

"Are you sure you're okay? You look like you've been spooked."

"I said I'm fine. I'll see you tonight." Before she could turn, he pulled her close and kissed her on the cheek. She smiled and walked out the door.

Stephanie's behavior bothered him, but he decided to leave it alone. He would see her later tonight and he was looking forward to spending some time alone with her.

Chapter Thirty-Eight

*D*onnie was on vacation. Every day he had scheduled activities with Kent and Jasper. He was going to save those boys, no matter what. He had grown to love them and wanted them to have a good life. Today, he was going to tell them he had filed to adopt them both. Since Stephanie had made it clear she would not return to him, he wanted to do something to help someone else, rather than to sit around moping.

He picked up Kent and drove to Jasper's foster home. When he arrived, Jasper came out. Car tires screeched to a sudden stop. As Donnie opened his door, a second car drove by and a hail of bullets rang out. Donnie was hit and so was Jasper. Kent was screaming and the foster mom called 911.

The ambulance and police arrived quickly. Jasper died at the scene. Donnie was shot twice and was barely hanging on. He was rushed to the hospital and Kent was taken by the policemen.

****

Stephanie went home and dressed for dinner. She knew it was a special occasion because Tony's was an exclusive place that folks went to for special occasions. The food and service were extremely expensive, and they didn't even pass out menus. If you had to see the prices, this was not the place for you. She dressed in a beautiful, black and white dress and black and white sandals. Her spirit was sad. She wanted to feel happy, but she was concerned about Daniel and whether he truly loved her or was using her as his trophy.

Before she left, she called to talk to Regina. When she picked up the phone, she confirmed that she would be arriving in the morning. "I cannot wait to see you. The last time you were here, I had to leave for the conference. This time, we'll find a chance to spend more time together. We have so much to discuss."

"Is everything okay, Steph? You sound somber." Regina listened.

"Things are okay. I just miss my friend and feel like I need you." She sat down on her bed. "My spirit is so weak. I just need to talk."

"Okay, babes. We will. I have to go back into the meeting to finalize some things so I can get on that plane in the morning. We will talk all day if you need to, and I will pray for you. Is that good?"

"Yeah. It is. You have my alarm information, so go straight to the house and I will be there around two o'clock." She exhaled.

"Sis, are you sure you're okay?" Regina's intuition gave off warning signs that something was wrong.

"All is well. I promise, we'll talk tomorrow. I don't want to hold you up, and it's not pressing."

They hung up the phone and Stephanie called her mom. "Mom, this is your daughter."

"I know who you are, but I cannot talk. I'm in with the doctor. Is everything okay?"

"Yeah, it's fine. Are you okay, Mom?"

"I'm getting my annual checkup, but the doctor just walked in. I'll call you later tonight, baby."

Stephanie grabbed her phone and left to go to the restaurant. She had a late meeting and promised to meet him at the restaurant. She arrived at 6:20 p.m. Grabbing the door handle, she hesitated and thought about leaving. But just as she turned around, Daniel touched her arm.

"Hey, sweetheart." He kissed her. "You were about to leave?"

"Hi, Daniel. I was about to go back to the car, but what I need is actually in my purse."

Daniel opened the door and they walked inside. He told the hostess their names, and they were guided to a private area in the back of the restaurant. Daniel pulled her chair out and she sat down.

"Thank you."

Daniel walked over and sat in his chair. "You're welcome."

They ordered their dinner. While they waited, they did a lot of small talk about many things. Daniel was so happy, and Stephanie tried hard to match his energy but things were off a bit with her.

He sensed it too, but decided not to force her hand at explaining what was going on with her. Their meals arrived and they ate.

"Thank you, Daniel. I love this place, and this lobster albanello is delicious. Thank you for inviting me here."

"Stephanie, anytime you want to come, just let me know. I will take you anywhere you want to go." He lifted the spoon to his mouth.

They ate in silence. When dinner was over, he asked if she wanted dessert, but she responded that she was full.

"Stephanie, I asked you here for a reason. Ever since I met you, I have had such happiness and feel we have a complete connection. I want to spend more time with you and share so much more of myself, my experiences, and travel with you."

"Daniel, what are you saying?" She was interrupted by the ringing of her phone. She stopped it from ringing and looked back at him.

"Stephanie, I'm asking you if you would— "

Her phone started ringing again.

"Please, just one second. I have to answer this call." She responded to the call. "What did you say?" She stood up. "Oh, my God, no. I'm on my way."

"Stephanie, what's going on?" Daniel stood up and walked to her side. She was hyperventilating and he was trying to calm her down.

"I'm sorry, Daniel. I have to get to the hospital. Donnie has been shot." She reached for her purse. He gently took her hand.

"Please, let me drive you. I'll pick your car up later."

"No, that's okay. I have to check on Donnie." She tried to leave but he retained her.

"Listen, you are too upset to drive. I'm taking you."

"Okay. Okay. Let's leave now, please." Stephanie was shaking and crying. It was as if she was losing the love of her life.

Pastor Winston felt like he lost the love of his, again.

Chapter Thirty-Nine

*T*hey arrived at the hospital and police officers, Donnie's family members, and friends were in the lobby. There were people wiping their eyes, and some were crying loudly. Stephanie ran over to Donnie's mom. "How is Donnie?" She was speaking fast and her voice was shaky.

"We don't know yet. He's in surgery." His mother blew her nose.

"What happened to him?" Stephanie was trying to be calm but her body was moving, and her legs were shuffling from side-to-side. Her body couldn't stop the rocking movement. "Please, tell me what happened."

"Someone shot him, sweetheart. That's all I can tell you." She turned to walk away then suddenly twisted back around. "Stephanie, Jasper died in the shoot-out."

Pastor Winston was standing near Stephanie, and when she heard that Jasper had died, she collapsed, falling into his arms. Daniel picked her up and took her to a more private area in the lounge and caressed her face until she became alert. "Daniel, please pray for Donnie and Jasper."

Bowing his head, he prayed until he felt a tap on his shoulder. "Mister Man, please pray for Mr. Donnie. If he dies, I don't know what I will do." Feeling God's power near, Pastor Winston assured the young kid, "He is not going to die."

Kent laid his head against Stephanie and cried himself to sleep.

He arrived at the hospital with his grandmother. Kent was so worried about Donnie, he cried to visit his mentor. They waited in the waiting room for five hours. Finally, the doctor came out and asked for Donnie's next of kin. His mother came forward, and they took her back. Stephanie asked his mother if she could accompany her, and she decided it might do Donnie good to see her there.

Pastor Winston asked God to direct his path. He didn't like seeing the woman he loved all broken down because of a past love. He was worried she might still have some feelings for him. He asked God to help him handle any problems he may encounter from this situation, and that God give him the strength to deal with the possibility that he might lose Stephanie.

****

Stephanie and Ms. Johnson entered the hospital room. Machines and equipment were everywhere. They were pumping fluids into Donnie's body, and there was a tube down his throat. He was unconscious. The doctor said that he had a 60 percent chance of making it. The bullet had missed some vital organs, but they were afraid he had lost too much blood.

Stephanie couldn't stand hearing the machines making all kinds of noises. It sounded like a pump room with beeping sounds and air being pushed through the machines. She couldn't take seeing him like that. Walking over to his bed, she took him by the hand. "Come back to us, Donnie. Please, come back. You can do this. We need you." She lay her head near his face. She needed him to know she was right there.

Ms. Johnson couldn't believe Stephanie was there acting like she loved her son. She had left him over one indiscretion. She only allowed her in the room to see her son because she believed it would help him? Although she had grown to love Stephanie, she couldn't help but be angry at the girl, who looked as if she was about to have a conniption over her son. She was sobbing and caressing him.

Ms. Johnson hoped that her soft touches on his skin would will him back. Her son loved Stephanie, so maybe by her being near him, willing him back, he would survive. She prayed Stephanie's presence would make a healing difference.

Pastor Winston called Elder Brown and asked if he could get someone to drop him off at the hospital. He explained the situation to him. He had promised Stephanie he would get her car back to her. Stephanie was so messed up when she received that call, that had he allowed her to drive, she could have had an accident. He wasn't willing to chance losing her. But as he stared into the room on the intensive care floor, and witnessed the woman he loved with her head lying next to her ex-fiancé's, rubbing and caressing him, he thought he needed to prepare himself for anything. This evening was a disaster, and it surely wasn't the way he planned it.

Chapter Forty

Sister Clay arrived at the True Church. She decided that nothing would keep her out of the church she grew up in during her early years. When she entered the doors, it seemed as if everyone had turned around and stared at her, but she would not be defeated. She had the right to worship wherever she wanted to and she would.

Pastor Davis was preaching, and the crowd was all riled up. The church had grown, and there were many people she didn't know. When she left the year before, there were about 2,000 members. Now, it seemed it was closer to 3,000. She took out her Bible to try to get into the sermon but she couldn't. She had a lot of anger and pain in her heart. Plus, she didn't like the pastor's wife.

She had known Denise Reese and her family for years. But since the girl left home for college and returned, she was nothing but a condescending, stuck-up, and un-Christian-like wannabe. She believed Denise had used her feminine ways to seduce the good pastor. She understood the devil sent Denise to the church to destroy it.

It was obvious this had happened, because Pastor Davis had changed. He was once a good man. But Denise was creeping in his bed, even though they both denied it. But she knew the truth because she had seen it with her own eyes. She saw Denise leaving his house bright and early one morning. That wasn't Christian behavior, and the girl was so disrespectful to her.

While the pastor was preaching, the images of Denise walking off his porch invaded her mind. She became angry. She couldn't hear his words or the message he was giving of hope and salvation. All she could think about was that he was a fornicating preacher. Suddenly, she stood up in the middle of his sermon and screamed, "Pastor Davis, you are going to bust hell wide open."

The sanctuary became eerily quiet. Almost everyone in the church turned to see who was making that noise and accusation. A deacon rushed over and forcibly removed her from her seat.

"Let me go, you heathen," she screamed, as she huffed and puffed. Sister Clay became violent and began to swing at the man. "Apparently, you don't know who I am."

"Sister, your outburst is unacceptable," the deacon said, as he ushered her out of the church. "Please, leave on your own, or we will have you removed by the law."

"I'm not going anywhere," she said, as she wiggled herself out of his strong hands. Sister Clay became verbally abusive and argued with the deacon. A member decided it would be best to call the police. It didn't take long for them to arrive and head into the church.

Sister Clay became louder and argumentative, as two officers walked into the vestibule.

"What's the problem?" the first officer asked.

"There's no problem. He's trying to make me leave. The law says I'm free to worship wherever I want to."

"But she's causing a problem, screaming stuff at the pastor during his sermon," the deacon said in frustration.

"What I'm saying is the truth." Pointing her finger in the face of the deacon, she said, "You know he shouldn't be in that pulpit. He is not worthy. He is absolutely not worthy."

"Come on, sister. Let's leave." The officer gently took her arm and pulled her toward the exit.

"Don't you touch me," she hissed. "I can walk out myself."

Sister Clay marched out the building with her chest poked out. She was not about to let them know that she was upset that she couldn't freely worship at her home church. "They can't get rid of me. I'll be back."

The police officers escorted her to her car and watched as she pulled off the parking lot and left the area. After assuring she was gone, they left the church.

Sister Clay waited until church was over and returned when everyone was gone. She picked up a brick and threw it through the beautiful, stained window. When she saw what she had done, she picked up another brick and busted the second window. Watching the windows crack and break into small pieces gave her a release of stress. The alarm sounded loud. Suddenly, she felt better and much stronger. It was the breakthrough she needed. She rushed and got into her car. "I didn't like what that pastor was preaching anyway. I don't have to worship where I'm not wanted." She sped off the parking lot, vowing never to return.

Chapter Forty-One

*P*astor Winston could not stop thinking about Stephanie. He picked up his cell and called her several times, but she didn't answer the phone. He wanted to get up and go to the hospital but realized he needed to give her space.

He was concerned about her welfare, so he called to check on her, but as usual, she didn't answer. He and Elder Brown drove her car to the hospital, and they prayed with the family and over Donnie. Pastor Winston's pride suffered from finding Stephanie still at the hospital. Five days later, she sat in the same spot near Donnie's bed, and it appeared she hadn't stepped a foot in her house. Though her clothes were different from the last time he laid his eyes on her, he felt she was changing at the hospital. He noticed a small suitcase that stood out in the room.

Upset over the events of this last week, he confided in his friend, Elder Brown. "I thought we shared something special." He shook his head. "Maybe I'm an old fool. Been so lonely for so long. I guess I fell in love too fast. I disappointed myself."

"Don't be hard on yourself. What happened with Stephanie is still painful for her. She probably needs more time."

"Are you kidding me?" Daniel stood up and paced the mauve-carpeted floor.

"No, I'm not. Maybe in her heart, there is still some type of deep, leftover, residual of love."

"We've been seeing each other a long time, and if she still wants him, maybe she likes the pain she suffered." The thought of her being in love with Donnie sickened him. "Why on earth would she want him back now?"

"I don't think she wants him back. She just doesn't want him to die."

"You're not making sense to me, nor is what she's doing."

Elder Brown ambled over to the pastor and stood in front of him. "Everything is not always as it appears. Maybe she is naturally concerned about him. Didn't he suffer the loss of a child he planned to adopt?"

"Yeah, he did." Pastor Winston sighed. "I feel so sorry about the situation. I wish Donnie well. Just not with the person I love." He rubbed his temple. "I'm stressed out. I never thought I would say that."

"You're dealing with your heart, brother, and the heart wants what it wants. Ain't nothing wrong with that, but a word of advice: don't push that woman too hard. She has been through something, and she needs to go through this to be sure. You should want to make sure her heart is yours. Let this play out." Elder Brown put his arm around his friend. "Give her a little bit of time."

"Yeah, I'll try." He picked up his Bible to leave. "I need this more than ever."

"Before you leave, please let me pray for you." Elder Brown prayed for his pastor and asked God to lead him and help him through this situation. He also asked God to heal Donnie and to work with Stephanie, so she would be free from strongholds, if that was what was happening with her. He asked God to guide and lead his friend, and if this relationship was not authored by God, to give his friend the strength to move forward, and to open his heart for what God set aside for him.

After the prayer, Pastor Winston left. He intended to go home and relax but his heart wouldn't let him. The desire to fight for the woman he loved proved too powerful. He realized that God would provide if he asked. The Bible said, if you asked, you would receive; and if you knocked, the door would be opened. Pastor Winston loved that Bible verse; Matthew 7:7. Deciding to stop everything he was doing, Pastor Winston turned his car around and headed straight back to the hospital. Stephanie would have to tell him herself, she was no longer interested in him. But until that time, he was going to fight for her love.

He turned his car into the parking lot and went directly to Donnie's room. He saw Stephanie standing over Donnie, whispering to him. She looked up and saw him. Stephanie smiled and walked toward the pastor.

"Hi, Daniel."

"Hey, Stephanie." He bent down to kiss her on the lips, and she allowed it but moved away quickly. "Is he coming around?"

She took him by the hand and guided him out of the room. "Yes. He woke up today. But they are still watching him. Although the bullets missed his heart, his stomach was damaged, and he lost a piece of his lung. But the doctor said he would be able to resume normal activities."

"That's a great blessing." Pastor Winston looked around to see if anyone could hear them. "I miss you, Stephanie. When are you going home?" He was hesitant to press her.

"Soon as I know for sure."

"Stephanie, you said he was going to be okay. I know he was your fiancé, but don't you think you're misleading him?" He grabbed her hands and gently caressed them.

She released her hands from his grip and backed up. "Please don't tell me you're jealous. He's my ex. But I have a past with him."

"I know that. But you have a present with me. I miss you."

"I miss you too, but I need you to be patient and give me some space." She turned to walk away.

"Stephanie, why do you need space?"

"I just do. Please, not now. I cannot do this now." She backed away and left him standing in the hall alone.

He didn't understand how he'd lost her. This situation wasn't good, and he felt so confused. When, how, and why had things gone so wrong?

****

Tabitha was having a hard time concentrating. Her thoughts were running rampant in her head. Constant ideas and information was traveling so fast, she couldn't keep up with what was happening. Her mom called to check up on her and couldn't understand what she was saying.

"Hey, Mom," she slurred, holding her words longer than their syllables allowed. "What you calling me for?"

"I was concerned about you," Mary Ann said. "It's been months since you stopped by and I need a favor from you."

"Yeah? That's the only time you call. So, where is your man? What are you doing? Are you drinking? Using drugs or what?" Tabitha flopped down on the couch and a puff of dust exploded in the air. She'd been so concerned about Donnie, she neglected to clean her small space for months, and she could smell the rotten food in the trash. There was stuff dumped into the garbage can so long ago, she couldn't remember when. She swatted flies circling everywhere. "Now you want something from me when all my life you have ignored me and treated me badly?"

"That's not true, Tabitha. I did what I could with what I had."

"What about the men, Momma? You know, the ones that raped me? You allowed that to happen." Tabitha couldn't help it. Her mind flooded to the many times she was molested, while her mom was laid out drunk somewhere. This just made her angrier. She wept.

"Baby, you have to understand. I lacked information about that stuff." Her mother took a swig of gin.

"You're drinking now, aren't' you?" She stood up and walked her sticky floor. As she walked in circles, her feet slammed against the tile, grabbing her shoe and refusing to release it. She used all her strength to pull her shoe back up with force. Too many times she spilled her overly-sweet Kool-Aid and failed to mop it up. She was so concerned about her relationship with Donnie, she allowed her life to go to poop.

"You knew. I told you." Tabitha screamed so loud it hurt her ears. "I told you. I told you." She kept repeating those words, as she cried.

"I don't remember. Are you going to give me some money? My rent is due." Her mother coughed, and it sounded as if the liquor she drank missed her throat and went down too fast, causing her to sound like she was being strangled.

"I hope you pass out. I'm not giving you anything. You have never done anything for me except destroy my life." She ended the phone call.

Tabitha glanced around her trailer and became disgusted. She must convince Donnie that they were good for each other. He loved her, and she knew it. She just needed to remind him.

She picked up her cell and called him again. The phone went to voicemail. This just made her upset. She had left his house in a hurry a week ago, because he had called the police on her. But she needed him to understand how much he loved her.

She grabbed her notebook and wrote down some new codes. She needed to decipher what he was really trying to say to her. She read the codes again. It said, 'please come over. I love you, Tabitha.'

"Yes, indeed. My man wants me back. I said that," she yelled. Just like she thought. He still loved her. She grabbed her notebook and her keys and rushed out of the trailer. She tripped on the torn carpet by the door and fell, head first, into the glass pane inside of the door, knocking herself out.

****

Mary Ann stumbled to her car, reeking of liquor. She jumped into her 1997 Buick Impala and tried to start her car by pressing the accelerator. She needed a new car like she needed another bottle of gin. But without a cent to her name, she planned to retrieve some from her only child.

She realized that the older she got, the harder she worked to captivate guys to pay for things. Since her beauty had faded, and the spring chicken that once existed flew the coup, she lived to talk some sense into that lying daughter of hers. Although Mary Ann realized drinking liquor caused her many problems, she believed her daughter had seduced her boyfriends, which is why she didn't believe her daughter. Tabitha lied to her on many occasions, just because she didn't like some of the men who visited.

Her mother assumed she lied because some of those times she accused the men, they were wrapped tightly together in bed, so her daughter's allegations were not truthful. Mary Ann believed once you told lies, it transpired into the adage of the girl who cried wolf when the dangerous animal did not exist. So, she supposed when Tabitha screamed a wolf hurt her, no one would believe her, and unfortunately, that is what happened with Tabitha.

Mary Ann patted the accelerator again before she realized her foot was repeatedly pressed on the brake.

"Darn," she hollered. "I gotta be more careful."

The car started after several false starts. "Where is my new sugar daddy? Momma needs a new car," she whispered.

Chapter Forty-Two

*R*egina was worried about her best friend. Her normal disposition disappeared. She wondered why she was staying at the hospital acting all broken over her two-timing, ex-fiancé. This behavior did not sit well with her, because Stephanie's sophistication, and sometimes bougie attitude refused to exhibit such negative conduct. Something else bugged her friend, and today, she was going to find out exactly what.

Regina stayed at Stephanie's house the entire week, and her friend stayed posted up at the hospital. She believed she was depressed. She refused to eat, cried all the time, and kept the hospital curtains closed.

Stephanie exhibited the same behavior once before, when they were in college, but she snapped out of that when confronted. Years ago, when Stephanie found out her first love was messing around on her, the poor girl's heart couldn't take it. She cried and retreated to her apartment and wouldn't leave it for weeks. They were freshmen in college, and it was her first, real relationship. He was the guy whom Stephanie lost her virginity to, with resistance because she pledged celibacy and hated to commit fornication, but Terrance pressured her, and against her will, she gave in. Stephanie believed Terrance was the one, and when she found him in his dorm room in bed with another girl, she went berserk. She was screaming and throwing things, and some sorority sisters forced her out of the men's dorm before she was kicked out of college.

The problem Stephanie suffered centered in betrayal, which

caused her to cry. Looking like a fool was not a characteristic she wanted to display to the world. It took a lot of praying and tears to gain her self-respect back and to return to her old self. That relationship changed Stephanie. She decided not to become serious with anyone else, and up until she met Donnie - her second, serious relationship - she lived up to her promise. Finding out about Donnie and that Tabitha girl devastated Stephanie because it took her back to her past hurt. She returned to church and met the good pastor. Regina recognized he was the real deal and she figured Stephanie loved him. But Stephanie appeared frightened and withdrawn, and Regina was committed to finding out why her best friend was hiding out in the hospital, acting all devastated about a man she no longer loved. What was eating Stephanie? What happened that she was hiding and running from the man she loved?

Today, she was going to find out and help her friend. She would not allow her to lose the one man she determined her friend loved. Something sent her heart packing, and it was up to her best friend to take that bag off the carousel and deliver Stephanie back to the land of the living.

Regina freshened up the house and washed the dishes and dusted the furniture. She laid her clothes out and took a shower. With three days left in town, she planned to spend them with Stephanie, and she was not leaving town until Stephanie and Daniel were back in each other's arms. They both deserved to be happy, and with God on her side, she was going to assure they followed their divine orders.

There was nothing like love, and what she witnessed happening with Stephanie and Daniel was something so beautiful, that she hoped to find it in the guy she was dating. True love was hard to find, and when you had it, you worked hard to keep it. Stephanie was hurting and acting strange and Regina was determined to find out why one way or another.

****

Four hours later, Regina entered the hospital, bringing Stephanie some fresh clothes. She strutted through the door and noticed Stephanie wiping tears away from her eyes.

She walked over, whispered to her, and Stephanie stood up and walked out of the room with Regina.

"What's wrong, sweetheart?"

"Regina, you don't grasp what I've been through today. My heart is broken again. Why can't I find the happiness I seek?" She laid her head down on her friend's shoulder and cried. After several seconds, she pulled her head away from Regina's shoulder and noticed the wet spot she left there. "I'm so sorry for messing up your clothes with my tears. I'm such a mess, girl. All I do is cry and pray."

"Keep crying because you are letting out the pain. Keep praying because God has brought you this far and He will bring you farther." Wrapping her arms around her best friend, she encouraged her. "Now, tell me all about it."

Stephanie poured her heart out to her best friend. No stone was left unmoved, tears were shed, and the truth was told. She released all her pain out to her dear friend, and suddenly, she sensed the weight of pain lifted off her shoulders, and her burden seemed light. She was ready to go home and leave her past behind.

Chapter Forty-Three

*W*hen she decided to leave the hospital, she bade Donnie good-bye and promised him she would support him but explained that their time had passed. Although he was hurt, he realized she was right. As Stephanie kissed his cheek and pivoted to leave, Donnie called her name.

"Stephanie, you are going to make the pastor a jubilant man. I messed up, and I pray that I can someday find again what I lost. I took you for granted and didn't give you the respect you deserved, but I still loved you. I messed up with you, but after I was shot, I asked God to forgive me. Now, I'm asking you, Stephanie. Will you forgive me?"

Stephanie walked back over to his bed, bent down, and kissed his cheek. "Yes, I forgive you. I wish you so many blessings, Donnie."

Strutting to the door, she twisted her body around and stated, "If you stay on the side of God, He will provide. Take care of Kent."

Leaving out the door, she headed to her house. Once there, she took a shower, changed into something comfortable and called Daniel. The phone rang seven times, but he didn't answer. She waited to see if he would text her but he didn't.

She stopped trying to call him and figured out the weakness she was experiencing was coming from her being hungry. She wobbled as she walked and had to grab the table to steady her gait. She grabbed her head and bent down to settle the dizziness. She waited a minute until it subsided then she stood up and walked over to the kitchen and cooked herself a light meal. When she finished eating her baked chicken, mixed vegetables, and a small salad, she called Daniel again. He still did not pick up.

She decided to give him more time. After all, she had been focusing her attention on Donnie, and understandably, his pride suffered from the alienation she administered. She understood. He needed time, and she would give that to him.

Stephanie waited almost three days, and she still had not heard from him. She was becoming concerned. She picked up her cell and texted him. No response.

She was getting worried. In the months since she'd known him, he had always responded quickly to her calls or texts. This was so unusual. Her heart ached for him.

****

There is nothing like family. It had been two weeks since Stephanie had seen her parents. To deal with the rejection she was feeling from Daniel, she called her mom. Crossing her legs and rearing back into the plush sofa, she waited for her mom to answer.

"Hello," the voice said on the phone.

"Momma. How long has it been since we've seen each other? I miss you and Dad. What are you doing?" She relaxed and uncrossed her legs.

"Hey, sweetheart. It has been a while. We are simply too old to sit in the house letting time pass. Boredom causes problems. Enjoy your life." Joan stirred the cake mix.

"You're right, Mom. I'm so glad you and Dad are enjoying your life together." She smiled and stood up. "I want the kind of love you two share."

"Baby, Ben and I had to work hard for this love. There is nothing easy about living and loving. You must keep it fresh and exciting. With time, you will enjoy what God's plan is. You and the pastor's life are a part of the Almighty's plan. Daniel loves you. The proof is in his eyes... The way he looks at you."

"Well, I'm not too sure he loves me now. I ran him away, standing by Donnie's side." The tears leaked quickly down her face. "What if I've lost him?"

"I don't think so. He's a pastor. Not only that, he is licensed for this kind of stuff. I'm sure he was hurt, but his love will overcome that. Talk to him. He'll understand. But pray first. Remember, God is already in the mix. When two people are in agreement, God is in the midst."

"Okay, Mom. I'm coming over to visit you and Dad. I miss and love you."

"I'm sure your dad will be happy you're coming."

"Okay. I'll be there in an hour." She walked around the room to look for her purse.

"Remember, there is nothing God cannot do. If you love that man, you fight for him."

"I will Momma. I'll be there soon; and, Mom, I love you."

"I love you too. I can't wait to see you."

Stephanie rushed around the room, searching for her purse, but before she grabbed her keys, she called Daniel. When he didn't answer, she left a message. "Daniel, I miss you. We need to talk. I'm sorry. Please call me."

She waited and received no response or text message. Her heart pounded with sadness, but she was going to reel her man back.

Chapter Forty-Four

*M*ary Ann made it safely to Tabitha's place. Although she had been drinking heavily, she had no incidents making it safely through the traffic. Most of the time, she wouldn't be driving after drinking, but she wanted to see her daughter. She needed her help.

She stumbled up to the door and viewed the broken pane of glass. She stuck her hand through an open area and unlocked the door. When she walked in, Tabitha's frail body was laid out on the raggedy carpet. Mary Ann bent down and shook her and spotted the blood on her daughter's head. Tabitha moaned. She shook her again, "Tabby, wake up. Wake up."

"Where am I?" Tabitha twisted and turned. "Oh, God, my head. My head. What happened? It hurts so badly."

"Don't move. Let me call the ambulance." Mary Ann jumped up to look for her daughter's cell. "Where's your phone?"

"Mom, I'm fine. I'm not going anywhere." She rubbed her head and used her left arm to help push herself up off the floor. "I'm okay, Mom. I remember. I bumped my head."

"But you need a doctor to make sure you're okay. This cut is deep, and blood is everywhere."

"Tabitha walked over to the kitchen sink and turned the faucet's cold water on. She grabbed a towel and soaked it with the water. She folded it and put it on the cut. "Ouch!" She grabbed the sink to keep from falling. She was a little dizzy, but overall, she felt okay.

"How did you fall into the door? Were you drinking or did that dude push you?" Mary Ann put her hand on her hips and used the other to grab the back of the couch to keep from falling.

"Seems to me you're the only one drunk, and I doubt if Donnie pushed me. He can't push no one."

"Well, I recognize a stalker by their actions, and that's what you do to him when you call and keep going to his office, right? What's all this nonsense about you and him getting married? That man is not going to marry you. You meant nothing to him but his little—"

She didn't finish what she was about to say because Tabitha ran over and slapped her mother so hard she fell on the couch.

"Don't you ever say such a thing. It is because of you I am not with him. You let your men rape me. You were never there for me. You loved your drinking and men more than you ever loved me."

Tabitha began to walk the floor. She was mumbling and saying weird phrases. "He is my man. Donnie loves me, he told me, and yes he told me." She repeated herself to make sure her message was clear. "When he can, we will be together. He loves me. I love him. We are one, till death. Yeah, that's right, till death."

"What is wrong with you? That man ain't thinking about you." She rubbed her face where she was slapped.

"You need to start back on your medicine. This is all in your head."

"I don't need that mess. I threw it away. You are the one who needs the medicine."

She walked over to her daughter. "I need some money for my rent. My landlord is going to evict me. I owe two months of payments. I'm getting old, babe, and no one is paying like they used to."

"I don't understand. I need to decode what you are saying. Where is my code book?"

She raced through the trailer looking for her book, and when she found it, she continuously repeated, "You are saying I am getting married. Oh, yes. Donnie loves me. Yes, he does." Tabitha screamed, as if she hit a gold pot of money.

Reaching up and putting her arms around her daughter, Mary Ann said, "honey, I need to take you to the hospital. That code book is part of the problem. Every time you stop taking your medicine, you rush to that book. You don't have to break codes to understand what anyone is saying. Come here, baby. I'm sorry for what happened to you. Let me find you some help, please?"

Pushing her mom hard up against a wall, Tabitha stated, "I said there is nothing wrong with me." She hissed through gritted teeth. "I will not allow you to have me committed again. I'm not crazy."

"Nah, baby, you are not crazy. You are schizophrenic, but remember, it is treatable with medication. You were doing well. Let me help you."

Tabitha's voice became childlike, as she began to speak like a little, lost child. "Mommy, will Donnie come to visit me? Will my husband stay with me if I go to the hospital? I'm so tired, Mommy. I'm so tired. My head is twisting with so much mess."

"I realize you're tired. Let me call an ambulance and you can go to your husband. He loves you and will come to the hospital to be with you." She hated lying to her daughter, but it would be the only way to encourage her to go to the hospital. Mary Ann recognized her daughter's cellphone under the table, by the couch, and she picked it up and called the emergency number and asked for help.

"Mommy, please don't leave me, please. I need you." She walked into her mom's arms and cried.

"The ambulance is on the way. We are going to make you feel better, baby. I love you." She squeezed her daughter's shoulders.

"Call my husband and tell him where I'm going. Please, Mommy, call Donnie." Wiping the tears away, she stated, "I love him, Mommy."

"Yes, baby. I understand." She walked her daughter outside to greet the ambulance attendants.

Chapter Forty-Five

Stephanie and her parents ate dinner then retreated to the den to watch television. As they sat down, Joan asked Stephanie had she seen the YouTube video that Sister Clay had made about the True Church and Pastor James Davis and his wife, Denise.

"You need to see this video on YouTube. I was shocked. So many church members and others saw it. The number of folks is up to 300,000. Sister Clay is really sad." Joan loaded the video and they all waited for it to start.

"Look at this mess. I don't see how a woman who claims to be a Christian can malign the pastor the way she is doing. God is not pleased." Joan shook her head and hit play.

Sister Clay sat straight and looked directly into the camera. "I was a member of The True Church. The pastor, who is a two-timing devil, is not right. He pretends to be a Christian while he stands in the pulpit and acts all sanctified and holy, but he is a fornicator. He was sleeping with the church whore, and I witnessed this on a trip to Las Vegas. I caught them, so I bared witness to their sin. I am flabbergasted and wanted to warn you good Christians not to go to this church. God is so unhappy. Pastor Davis is not the only one who is playing with God. Most of the people are sinners and pretend to be so loving and kind, but they are the devil in disguise." Sister Clay stopped talking. She reached for a tissue from a box sitting close by and dabbed the tears running down her face. She acted like she couldn't go on.

Emotional, she bent her head into her open-palmed hand and boohooed. Finally, she lifted her head up and said, "He's not the only whore in the church. His elders sleep with as many members as they can. Those members are cold-hearted. Last year, two women got into a fight and were rolling around on the floor in the kitchen like dogs in heat. They were cussing and acting a fool. This is not a holy place." She dabbed her eyes again. "The woman who has the pastor acting like a pimp is not a Christian. She is a fake. Her name is Denise. That lady's reputation precedes her, and on good authority; she was messing around with a married man. If you do a search on Google, you will find that Denise was shot last year by a woman suffering from mental health issues in a big mess of people having affairs with each other. Yet the so-called, good pastor still made her First Lady." She stood up and walked closer to the camera. The church is located in East St. Louis. Go see for yourself. I would meet you there, but because I am all about truth, I was banned from the church and the premises. I thought we had the freedom to worship where we wanted to, but apparently, I was wrong. Help me remove these people. Flood their phones and demand this man's removal. He should not be standing in anyone's pulpit. I am Sister Clay. I'm not perfect, but at least I'm real."

"Wow." Stephanie sighed. That lady is crazy. What person in their right mind wouldn't be afraid to anger God with that mess? She is so filled with hate. That's so sad."

Stephanie's dad grunted. "She is allowing the devil to use her. She is doing his dirty work. But God will not allow her to win. You cannot win when you are playing dirty."

"Dad, I don't understand how she could do that. No matter how angry you become, I learned when I was a child, if you dig a ditch for someone else, you need to dig another one for yourself." Stephanie stood up and stretched. "What's bad are the comments. They are almost as bad as the video. People today fall for anything negative. I think God will make them accountable for what they spread around, as well as Sister Clay. She is leading people away from God, and He is not pleased."

"I packed you something to take home with you for later. You look pale and thin. Now, what's happening with you and the pastor?" Her mother walked into the kitchen. She washed pots and pans, and she worked diligently as the cookware clanked around. The rushing of water permeated the air. "Baby, girl." Her mother's voice rang out.

"Yes, mother?" Stephanie entered the kitchen.

"I want you to pray for the pastor. He loves you. But you've hurt him with your shenanigans by standing by Donnie. Donnie hurt you, but you used that pain to hurt the pastor, and that's not right." She walked further into the kitchen, opened the cabinets and reached for the plates. "Wash your hands and call your daddy to the table for dessert."

After eating dessert, they chatted. Stephanie made up her mind to be transparent with the pastor. "Momma, please pray for Daniel and me."

Her mom and dad circled her and prayed. Stephanie left the house feeling invigorated as if she was on the way back to happiness. She vowed nothing would keep her from her man.

Two days and 49 minutes after not hearing from Daniel, Stephanie entered the church. She wore an all-white, fitted dress that clung to every inch of her body. She was stunning. She had one thing on her mind, and that was to return her man back to his place in her life. He was standing in the pulpit preaching when she sauntered into the sanctuary. He was preaching, and she noticed the tears escaping his eyes and running down his cheeks. He was flashing across the large screens perched around the church. The view was so clear you could see every imperfection on his face. There were not many, but she noted the small scar he received when he was a little boy and fell off his bike.

He turned and watched her. Even though she wore a hat that slanted across her eyes, he could recognize that body and that walk anywhere. His heart pounded, as he tried hard to stay on message. She took a seat up on the second pew and stared at him. Eventually, he closed out the sermon because he could no longer concentrate.

After the benediction, he and the members of the pulpit went to their positions in the back of the church to greet the leaving congregation. Stephanie moved closer, and his heart beat faster.

"Pastor, I need to see you now, and I'm not leaving until I do."

"I'm busy right now. Make an appointment with my secretary." He tried to move her to the side so he could speak to the next member but she wasn't having it.

"Pastor, you don't want me to make a scene. I need to talk to you right now." The look in her eyes spoke words that he discerned she would say if he didn't comply. He excused himself and guided her to his study. Once inside the door, she started talking.

"You're disappointed. I'm sorry. I operated poorly in pain and refused to interpret what I was thinking, to act like Donnie meant more to me than you. But deep down, you recognized that's not true. I love you, and you internalized that."

"No, I didn't. It seems to me you care more about him than you do me. Therefore, please go and be with him. I pray for your happiness."

"Do you really think getting rid of me is that easy? You cannot push me away. I want you." She brought her body near his.

"I don't think so." He eased backward, stepping away from her beautiful body. She took his breath away, and he tried to catch it. His words caught into the air. "We can be friends. I can't give my heart back to you."

"What are you saying?" Stephanie took her hat off. It was in the way. "Please, tell me you don't mean that."

"But I do."

"So, just like that? You're letting me go?" She swiped the tears away. "I love you."

"Not enough, Stephanie. Now I need to leave." He pulled his jacket close and headed toward the door.

"You're not going to even ask me why?"

"No explanation needed. You showed me why. You didn't love me enough." He reached for the door.

"Then I'm glad you didn't get a chance to ask me to marry you. If you cannot handle something like this, I wouldn't want you to be my husband. You're too self-serving. You don't consider what could've possibly made me run from your proposal."

Now she pivoted to walk out of the room. "Thank God I found out you're not strong enough."

"How did you find out I was about to ask you to marry me?"

"What difference does it makes? You don't want me..."

"Please tell me who told you?"

"Nobody informed me. A woman's intuition is always on target." She walked out the door, but he pulled her back inside his office.

"If you believed that, why did you run back to him?"

She wiped her tears away with the back of her hand. "This is the truth. Sister Jamie Johnson told me you gave her your credit card when you took her to Vegas and bought her so many beautiful clothes. She said she has been sleeping with you until I showed up and broke you two up."

"What?" His hand flew up toward his forehead, and he tried to rub the stress away. "When did she tell you that?"

"The day I showed up for Bible study. She told me everything." She tried to suppress her groans of pain, but they seeped out.

He thought back to that day and how strange she had acted. "Stephanie, you're the only one that's held that card in their hand except for a cashier. What do you take me for anyway?"

"How would she know? She said so much, which I thought that only you and I had that information."

"Maybe she heard me discussing it with Elder Brown. I cannot believe this. All this time, I thought you didn't love me... but you thought I was in love with another woman."

"So, you're saying she lied?" Stephanie breathed a sigh of relief.

"Stephanie, I didn't date women in my church until you. There hasn't been anyone else, and if I had, it wouldn't be Sister Johnson.

She's not even my type." He scooted his body next to her and pulled her into his arms. "I love you. But if you want me, you have to marry me right now. No more games. I want you now."

"We don't have a marriage license. So, it wouldn't be legal."

"It will be legal in God's eye. We can go to the recorder of deeds Monday and get the official license. One of the pastors can marry us right now."

"If you're sure this is what you want to do, I'm okay with it."

"I am absolutely sure. I love and need you."

He kissed her, and once he released her, he said, "I'll be right back."

Daniel strutted out the door. His steps had a purpose. His feet slammed the carpet with an urgency. The covered floor released air as the sound vibrated throughout the room with loud squeaks from the pressure of his foot.

When Daniel returned, he was with eight people. Both sets of parents, Regina and Elder Brown, and Pastor Davis and First Lady Denise.

Chapter Forty-Six

Stephanie put her hat back on. She was already wearing all white. The pastor had on a black suit. They both stood in front of Pastor Davis, who decided to visit with his friend to encourage him. They had previously discussed Daniel's disappointments. His friend wanted to be with him in prayer. Pastor Davis and Denise were happy Stephanie came through the church doors, and he was happy to be of service to their friends. More than anything, he was pleased they were getting married. He knew that he who finds a wife, findeth a good thing, and that pleased his heart.

Everyone that Stephanie loved was standing in the pastor's study. Regina rode to the church with her friend, and waited in the car to determine what would happen before she came into the church. When Stephanie didn't come back out, she went in to support her. To witness the two lovebirds about to become one brought smiles to everyone's faces.

Stephanie was glowing. Her eyes were filled with tears that threatened to release themselves as they leaned over her bottom eyelashes. Daniel's tears ran down his face without shame or embarrassment. He had waited so long for a love like this. He patiently waited on God to fulfill his promises. As always, God was on time.

"Who gives this bride away?" Pastor Davis bellowed.

"I do," Ben responded.

As the ceremony continued, every face in the room shined with tears that trailed their faces. The ceremony was beautiful. Stephanie stared deeply into Daniel's eyes and whispered, "I love you so much."

"Me too." They both laughed.

"Now, that was funny. Do you love Stephanie or yourself, Pastor?" Regina asked with a soft giggle.

"That didn't sound right, but my baby recognized what I meant."

Pastor Davis finished the ceremony and said, "You may kiss your bride."

Daniel pulled Stephanie close to him and kissed her with passion. His stomach became weak and his heart rate increased. They hugged and kissed, forgetting others were in the room.

"Get a room," Regina said. The room of people laughed.

"That is the plan," Pastor Winston said.

Daniel whispered to Stephanie. "You can plan the wedding you want. I just couldn't go another day without you. I love you. Whatever you want, you can get it."

"We'll discuss that later." She reached up and wiped a tear spilling from Daniel's right eye.

"I present to you, Pastor Dr. Daniel and Stephanie Winston," Pastor Davis said with outstretched arms.

Stephanie reached up and hugged her best friend. "Regina, thank you so much for being here with me. If it weren't for you, this wouldn't have happened at this moment. Thank you for making me talk to him. I love you so much."

"I'm so happy. But remember, none of us could stop God's plan. He's able. We'll talk later."

"Mom, Dad, I love you both so much. Thanks for your patience with me. I'm so glad you were here today." She kissed her parents on their cheeks.

"We wouldn't have wanted to be anywhere else. We're so proud of you."

Stephanie squeezed Denise's hand. "We have so much in common. I'm so glad we are friends. I'm going to need you."

"I'm right here for you."

Stephanie hugged Daniel's beautiful mom, Charlotte, and his dad, Daniel, Sr. "You both have raised a wonderful and faithful son, I'm so proud to be his wife. Thank you so much for being here today. I enjoyed the time I spent with you both in D. C."

"We are so happy Daniel has found love. We wish you nothing but happiness and grandkids, as well," his mother said with a brilliant mouth of white teeth. Everyone in the room laughed.

Stephanie hugged his parents and Daniel thanked his parents for being there at this time with him. Unbeknownst to Daniel, his parents and friends surprised him this morning. He wasn't expecting them, but he realized that God was the author of everything. Stephanie and Daniel mingled a while and thanked everyone, and after about 30 minutes, Daniel announced he was taking his bride home.

"I thought we could all go to dinner," Regina said.

"Let's plan a special dinner for Friday. But right now, I just want to be with my wife. Momma Joan, would you and my mom do that for us? That way, my other family members can come and be with us. And, Mom, I'll call you at the hotel later.

Turning to Stephanie, he informed his bride, "Stephanie, my siblings will be disappointed they are not here to accept you into our family, but they will be here next Saturday, and we can all celebrate again."

"They'll understand. We've been fighting so many fires we haven't had time to spend with your entire family. But we will."

"We better get home. We'll talk more there." He reached for her hand and guided her out of the office.

"Don't hurt her, Pastor," Elder Brown laughed.

Pastor Winston smiled and guided his wife through the door.

****

Sister Green picked up her phone and called Sister Clay. She wanted to tell her about the YouTube video and how God wouldn't be pleased. Sister Clay answered the call after the third ring.

"Sister Clay, I was calling to speak to you today about what I saw. But first, Happy Monday to you."

"Sister Green, ain't much to be happy about on this Monday morning." She coughed and grunted.

"Anytime you are on this side of the dirt, that's something to be joyful and thankful to God for his goodness and kindness."

"Whatever. But what do you want?" Her voice was cold and flat.

"No need to be huffy with me. I wanted to discuss that video you put up on YouTube. I don't think you have made God proud. You posted lies and untruths, and you know how God feels about that." She took a deep breath.

"Who said they are lies? You don't know what I know. You're like those sanctified sitting ducks in the church. You sit there acting like nothing happened and don't do jack when the church members are messing up."

Taking a deep breath that brought out a loud puff of air from her mouth, Sister Green spoke. "You're right about that. I have not been truthful. I should be honest and I'm going to do that right now. You should be ashamed of yourself. You have not acted like a Christian in the past five years. I'm not sure what you're going through. I don't know if you're depressed, or suffering from an illness, but we have failed you. Whatever I can do to help you, I want to be there for you."

"There is nothing wrong with me. But you overbaked, set in your ways, fake Christians need to repent. You knew Pastor Davis and that girl was sinning, and none of you did a thing. I was the only person that confronted them." She patted her fingers on the kitchen counter.

"I'm sorry you feel that way. None of us know what happened with that couple. Only God knows, and only He will judge. They were baptized and confessed their sins, and that's what God asks us all to do. Who are you to crucify them and to try to shame them? You have no right. You should be praying for them, but instead, you are doing everything you can to harm them. Please stop and save your soul. They have done what God asked. Now you should too."

"Well, I'm not taking that YouTube video down. I'm making so much money with all those views." She giggled and tried to contain her laughter by covering her mouth. The sound was muffled, but you could still clearly catch the vibration bouncing from the volume.

"You know there are many people in this world who love to listen to gossip and are very messy. So yes, you'll get a lot of views. The sad part is you will lead a lot of people from God with that mess. You cannot win souls being messy," she mumbled. "Lord, help us."

"I heard you, sister, and the Lord is helping me. I'm getting a check without doing anything. I need that money."

"All money is not good money. You reap what you sow." Sister Green was getting nowhere with Sister Clay, and she was getting frustrated. "You know, sister, we are charged to show people to Jesus, not to run them away. In Mark 11:25, God commands us: And when ye stand praying, forgive, if ye have ought against any: that your Father also which is in heaven may forgive you your trespasses."

"Girl, that doesn't mean what you think." She grunted while walking backwards and forward in her kitchen.

"Sister Clay, basically, if you want God to forgive you, you have to forgive others. If you want to heal from all this stuff going on, forgive and repent. Let God use you to do His work."

She took a deep breath to pull in the air she released when she made her statement.

"Like I said, I will pull it when I'm good and ready. If this call is over, I'm about to hang up and go spend some of the money I made from the commercials on my YouTube page." She did a little high kick into the air.

Sitting down to rest her weary legs and her soul, Sister Green said, "Sister Clay, may I pray for you?"

"You pray while I keep getting these checks from YouTube."

"No, sister, but if you want me to pray for a financial blessing from God, and that you remove that video, I will."

"Are you for real? There is no way I'm going to allow you to pray for me. You are on the team of sinners, so your prayers are not reaching the Almighty." She took her finger and pushed the phone keyboard. "Can you hear me now? Can you hear me now?"

Sister Green quickly got the message and hung up. She didn't want to hear the keyboard booming in her ear as Sister Clay played with the keyboard letters. "Lord, help Sister Clay. I do not want to see my sister in Christ lost. We all have our burdens and heartaches. I believe Sister Clay needs your counsel and counselors here on earth. Something is hurting her, which is probably why she is hurting others. I also ask that you build a coat of armor on Pastor Davis and his wife. This couple is working hard in the church for you, and you can see it by the growth of the church. Lord, you have blessed them with over five hundred new members in two years, and even with that negative video, it's leading folks to the church. Even if they don't realize that what was made for bad against this family is reaping good memberships and more people working on behalf of You. I pray that Sister Clay put away her bitterness and seek counseling to heal her heart. Thank You, Lord, for being the God who forgives, the God who loves us even when we do wrong. Thank You so much for Your favor. I ask You this in Your name. Amen."

Chapter Forty-Seven

onnie walked into the hospital chapel to pray and give thanks to God for saving his life. He knew that had it not been for God's grace, he would not have survived the bullets entering his stomach. He was so grateful, and he wanted to thank God for being so good and merciful to him.

As he bent before the altar, he whispered, "Thank You, God. You have brought me through so much. I'm sad about the loss of Jasper. He was a good, young boy who was trying to get his life right. He had so many obstacles, but he was trying. Please, Lord, bless his soul. He was so young. He had just turned twelve, so I pray that You will be merciful to him. I heard that kids cannot be responsible for their ways and will not be judged before their thirteenth birthday. I pray that's true. Thank You for blessing and saving little Kent. I promise to do right by him and give him a better chance at life than Jasper had. Thank You and help me to grow more spiritually. Amen."

Next, he went to get his clothes out of the hospital room and was told by the nurse that he had to wait for the hospital transporter to take him down to exit out of the hospital. "Nurse, I don't need any help going to my car. As a matter-of-fact, my mom is already here and she can walk with me."

The nurse politely completed the paperwork she was writing on the clipboard and handed it to Donnie. "I need to explain your dis- charge information to you, and I will need your signature after you review it. By the way, it is the hospital policy that patients be transported down by our staff. If you want to leave, you must comply."

"I understand. But I don't need the help."

"Son, just do as the nurse instructs," his mom said.

"It's our policy." Then the nurse read the information to him and explained the discharge summary for him. "Do you understand?"

"Yes. I do. I don't think you will have to worry about seeing me again," he said with a smile, as he signed one of the forms acknowledging the receipt of the information about the discharge procedures and gave it back to her.

Taking the form and attaching it to the clipboard in her hand, she said as she twisted around, "I'll be right back with the transporter."

Donnie turned to his mother and stated, "You sure do have to go through a lot to leave this place."

"Yes you do, son, but the blessing is that you are leaving in one piece and that God has blessed you with good health, after all that happened to you."

"It is a blessing; and trust me, I know it, and I won't forget it."

"How's little Kent doing?" His mother stood as the transporter walked into the room.

"Excuse me, sir," the transporter pushed the wheelchair over so that Donnie could get in.

"Are you kidding me? I have to leave in this?" He stood up from sitting on the bed.

"Yes, sir. It's the hospital's policy."

Donnie sat in the wheelchair and turned to his mother. "Little Kent is doing great. I cannot wait to see him and explain what the future holds for him."

His mother walked behind the transporter as he pushed her son. "That little, young man is a special blessing. He has a beautiful spirit about him. I love spending time with him."

"So do I, Mom. I love that little boy. I pray I can spend more quality time with him."

They reached their car that the valet brought to them after his mom gave him her ticket. "Trust me, Mom, if I get my way, you will see more of the little fella."

Donnie stood up and got into the passenger side of the car. His mom walked over and gracefully got into the driver's seat. She waited until the transporter shut her door and drove off. "Son, you have been through some things. I want you to use your pain to become stronger, to love and live your life to the fullest. God has been so good to you. You have mentored these young men, and I'm proud of you. You must continue to make a difference. In doing so, you must respect relationships."

"I have learned that the hard way. I lost the love of my life trying to have it all." He leaned his right shoulder on the car's door and looked in the direction of his mother.

"Well, son, God doesn't make mistakes, but we do. If we live through the errors, we can always get better. Though I love Stephanie like a daughter, she was not your soul mate...Not the one God chose for you."

"You're wrong, Mom. I loved her." He twisted in his seat and tried to scratch his back.

"It's not enough to just love her. That's why I know she was not who God chose for you and you were not who He chose for her. If God had been involved in the mix, you wouldn't have needed someone else. She would have been enough." His mother, Connie, looked ahead. "God gives us enough. I do believe He will give us more. But He does know our needs, and Stephanie was not yours."

"I hate hearing that. Especially, since I cared so much for her." He lifted his finger and wiped a lone tear that released from his right eye.

"Son, if you allow God to do His work, He will direct your path. He promised us that in the Bible. In Proverbs 3:6 it says, 'In all thy ways acknowledge Him, and He shall direct thy paths.'" She smiled at him. "Your life will change if you allow God in."

Donnie sat and listened to his mom. All his life his mom had lived a Christian lifestyle. He knew she was a believer and she taught him and his siblings to love God. Along the way of growing up and becoming an adult, he stopped going to church. But after all, he had been through, he felt God had given him a second chance. He planned to make the best of his new life.

Chapter Forty-Eight

Tabitha stood staring out the window of her new home. She had spent the past two weeks living in the godawful place. Although, she could admit that she felt much better. She also felt confined and sad. She missed Donnie. She believed that he would be her savior and save her from her drab life. But she had concluded, with the doctors and the psychiatrists that she had to help herself. They encouraged her that she could do better and that with the right medication, she could live a normal and productive life. Also, they were going to help her navigate her way back into society.

Her mother had promised to stop drinking and had started going to an Alcoholics Anonymous support group. Her mom had told her she had not had a drink in 10 days. That was an excellent start for a person who had been drinking for a lifetime.

Both Tabitha and her mom had been through some trauma in their lives, and because it was never addressed properly, they just continued with their lives with so much pain, they took on more baggage, never getting better. Tabitha realized that without counseling and support, she could have died. She was thankful. As she stared out into the parking lot, a knock on the door interrupted her thoughts.

It was her mom. "Hi, baby," Mary Ann whispered loud enough for her daughter to hear but soft enough to soothe her. She walked over and kissed her on her left cheek.

"Hi, Mom." She turned and looked at her. "Mom," she roared.

"You look great." She rubbed her hands through her bouncy hair. "What have you done to yourself?" Her daughter's face was beaming with joy.

"I know it's only been two weeks, but things are changing for me. I'm living in a residential treatment center, working, and they have a hairdresser that comes on site and she fixed my hair and made up my face. I feel like a different person. Plus, we go to the chapel daily, and I've found God."

"Mom, you look so good. I'm so proud of you." She took her mom's hand and they walked over to the couch in her room. They sat down on the gray-looking, used sofa. "We are both getting better. It's a shame it took a failed relationship to get us here. I never thought my life could get better. Although I know it's too early to celebrate, I do feel like I'm heading in the right direction. I had refused to take medication, but now I know that even with a diagnosis of schizophrenia, I can still live normally with medication."

"That's why I kept telling you to stay on your medication. There is nothing wrong with having a disorder. The problem occurs when you don't stay on your medication. With medication, you can still live a normal life, work, and do everything else. You just have to allow the medicine to work for you." She brushed a wisp of hair behind her beautiful daughter's ear. "Honey, you are so gorgeous. I remember when I looked just like you. I felt so beautiful. But I was so unhappy."

Tabitha squeezed her mom's hands. "What happened to you, Mom? All my life, you've been miserable and drinking. That affected me. I couldn't help you." Tears dropped from her eyes. "I wanted to, but you pushed me away."

"I was raped so many times by people who were supposed to protect me. My uncles, cousins, neighbors, and my mom's friends. No one would believe me, so I drank to stop the pain. My mom didn't protect me. So, I didn't know how to keep you safe. I promised myself I would not allow what happened to me to happen to you. But I failed you, darling. I'm so sorry. Please accept my apologies." Mary Ann laid her head into her hands and allowed her loud cries to ring out into the room. Her moans vibrated off the high ceilings, and Tabitha's voice danced off the wall, as she responded to her mother's testimony.

"Mom, I was so angry and disappointed in you. I believed you didn't protect me because you didn't want to. Now, I know, through counseling, that if trauma is not dealt with when it happens, it can do more damage later. You couldn't protect me because you didn't know how. Don't beat yourself up. Let's stay in counseling so we don't pass this stuff on to the next generation."

"Oh God, thank You. How did I become so blessed when I have always thought God had abandoned me?"

"I felt the same way. But the truth is, we kind of abandoned ourselves. We stayed in unhealthy relationships, used people to get what we wanted, played games with each other, and so much more. Even though we knew better, we used people to achieve our means."

"Why did we wait so long for help?" Mary Ann asked, as she took her hand and wiped the sweat beads that popped out on her forehead. "This morning in the chapel, they sang this song saying you can't hurry God, you just have to wait. But the song was saying that God will come, and when He does, He's always on time. I'm so glad God arrived. I was at my wit's end. I wish someone had introduced me to God again sooner. I gave up on him when I was a little girl. I believed He didn't protect me. But so far, I'm learning through reading the Bible, He really did. He brought me through it. We are all going to go through a lot of pain, but we must push through, pray and allow God to use that pain to make us better."

Tabitha hugged her mom and squeezed into her small frame. "I love you, and I will do everything to live right, to be healthy, and to keep God in my life. Let's do this together. We can do this, Mom."

"With God, all is possible. We are going to make it, baby. I love you."

"I love you too, Mom."

Chapter Forty-Nine

*S*ister Clay pulled into the parking lot of her old church and observed the tall structure. Tears streamed down her face as she remembered the many good times she had there. The longer she stood flat foot and stoic, the more her heart pained. She became upset that it had come to this and that she had to part from the church she once loved. It had been her family's church for years. Sister Clay remembered the children she taught in Sabbath School and the activities she planned for the young people. She was proud of everything she did to help people to love God and to give themselves to Him.

As the tears leaked and cascaded down her face, she wiped them away. Her eyes became blurry, and she struggled to see through the haze her tears left behind. She didn't understand what happened. She didn't want to be lost, and she surely didn't want people to see her as a troublemaker.

It all started with that Denise Reese. She was once her daughter's friend. Denise left town for college and didn't often return to her hometown. Prior to her growing up, they had a great relationship. She taught her in Sabbath School and had also taught her how to act in the plays she had written for the young people. But when Denise returned to the church many years later, she was different.

Denise was young, wealthy and beautiful. As Sister Clay aged, she didn't feel so pretty or accomplished. After her husband had left her to pick up the pieces and to care for the family, Sister Clay became bitter. She didn't mean to have such an ugly attitude, but some folks just brought that out of you. There were arguments in the church, and some fights, and Sister Clay had always been involved in them. Maybe she did run her mouth too much, but so what? Other people gossiped and talked just as much. There were people in the church having affairs, stealing from the poor funds, and taking food from the food pantry that was intended for the poor. But everyone watched her and blamed her for every single thing that went wrong.

She was sorry she had accused the pastor and Denise of having premarital sex. But she saw Denise and Pastor James Davis as sinners. She saw Denise, with her own eyes, exit the pastor's house early one morning. Why would she be leaving that time of morning if they weren't sinning? The only thing Sister Clay did was expose them. Telling everyone about them just set off a chain of negative responses. But still, Sister Clay felt vindicated until the good, old pastor married that hussy.

She wiped her tears, as she recalled the mess that occurred at the church she once called her home. But she would cry no more. Since she posted that video, it had already hit ten million views. She was making money and was about to do what she should have done a long time ago. Today, she decided to start her church. Yes. That's exactly what she planned to do. No one would put her out of her church. She was going to buy her a building, recruit some members, and become a pastor. A smile crept across her face. Her eyes glistened with fresh tears. God had given her the answer she needed to hear. She was going to build it, and the members would come. She was so excited that she tossed around several names to see which would make more sense. The Good People's Missionary Baptist Church, Saint Clay's on the Mount, and Redemption Baptist Church were some of the names popping around in her head. She saw some young people come out of the church and she approached them with a smile.

"Hello, young ladies. I'm starting my church and I would love for you all to visit. We'll do so much, and you all will have the freedom to participate and plan programs and do what you want. Don't you think that would be a good thing?"

The young people's eyes beamed. "We could do whatever we want?" One girl asked.

"Yes, as long as we don't displease God. But yes, I will give you a freedom you don't have here. But don't mention it to anyone. I will get back with you all once I open the doors of the church. I want you all to think about how you want the church to be."

"That sounds exciting. Let us know when." The young group of girls walked away smiling.

Sister Clay looked up to the heavens and said, "Thank You, God. I got this, and nobody can stop me now.

Chapter Fifty

*D*aniel and Stephanie arrived at the courthouse to pick up a marriage license. They were ready to make their marriage official in the eyes of the law. Although they had married with ordained pastors, they wanted to ensure all was well as the state law mandated.

Finally, they were happy. They had gone through so much to find the love they were experiencing, and were giddy like teenagers. Stephanie draped her arms around her husband's waist, and he kissed the top of her head. Pastor Winston was so happy he had waited on God to send him the woman of his dreams. He couldn't be any happier than he was this day. "Baby, I'm so happy right now, and I pray that God will allow us to experience this happiness forever."

"He will. We can make sure that happens. We just have to trust each other, communicate, and stay close to God. Everything will work itself out. Let's promise to love and honor each other."

Pastor Winston took his arms from around his wife's neck and turned her to face him. "I love you, Stephanie, with my heart and soul. I promise to remain faithful, honest, to pray with you, and stay close to God. He brought us to each other, and He will carry us through." Daniel pulled his bride close to him and passionately kissed her.

Stephanie's legs wobbled, and she almost lost her balance. But the man she loved tenderly pulled her up to him. She stood on her toes and kissed him. "I love you, Daniel. You make me happy. I have never experienced a love like this and pray daily that God will allow us to enjoy each other for as long as our hair turns gray and our minds age together. I want to spend my life loving only you."

Daniel kissed her tears away. "If we remain faithful to God, we can survive anything together." They held hands, squeezed them together, and strutted confidently into the courthouse to apply for an official marriage license. As they stood at the counter, Sister Clay walked in.

"Hi, Pastor. How are you and your lady?" She smirked as she talked. "What are you two lovebirds doing here in the courthouse?" She leaned against the counter and stared in their direction.

"The question is, why are you here?" Pastor Daniel threw the question back to her.

Sister Clay laughed. "You will find out soon enough." Then she walked over to the counter and asked the lady could she speak in private, away from the couple standing too close to her. She was there to pick up a license for property.

Pastor Daniel and Stephanie got what they came for and left without looking back. They were happy and planned to stay that way. They would allow no weapon that was formed against them to prosper. They wrapped their arms around each other, gazed into each other's eyes, and walked out of the courthouse.

Epilogue

Stephanie stood at the microphone singing on Sabbath morning with the praise team, as the pastor, program participants, and deacons walked into the sanctuary to take their place in the pulpit. Pastor Daniel Winston looked for his bride in the choir. They caught each other's eyes, and he winked at her. She blushed with pride.

They were celebrating six months of marriage and they were happy. She spent her time in the church working with the women's ministry team, singing in the choir, and working as the church clerk. She had promised herself to work in close collaboration with her husband and to be a true helpmate to him. Life was good. The church was growing, and the Spirit was high.

Donnie was sitting in the audience with his son, Kent. He was also seriously dating a young lady he had met years ago in college. They had become reacquainted when he adopted Kent. She was the lawyer who had helped him with the paperwork and represented Donnie and Kent in court. Before service started, Pastor Winston and Stephanie had spoken to Donnie. Donnie explained that Kent just wanted to see Stephanie and to thank her for everything she had done for him when she was spending time with Donnie. He wanted her to know he had become a son. They hugged, and Donnie introduced Stephanie to his fiancée. Donnie said he had no plans to return to Pastor Winston's church, but just wanted to thank Stephanie for being there for him. He also asked her for forgiveness and said he was saved.

Stephanie sang her heart out. God had inspired her, and she knew that whatever you asked for in His name, He would provide. He had fulfilled His promises to her. She never dreamt the day that voice had led her to this church, that it was God protecting her and sending her to her destiny. The devil tried to kill her, but God saved her from sin, from dying without knowing Him and from living without finding her soul mate, the man God had chosen for her. Tears dripped onto her white shirt, leaving a trail of wet spots. The pain she was filled with felt like her body was imploding when she drove erratically onto the church grass and rushed into the church screaming for the pastor. She had no idea she was there to find her husband, Daniel, the man who would comfort her and teach her about God's love. She smiled and looked up to heaven as she sang, "I Surrender All." She had surrendered to God, and all was good.

CPSIA information can be obtained
at www.ICGtesting.com
Printed in the USA
LVOW03s2137240118
563863LV00014B/73/P